W9-BFE-795

WALK SOFTLY

AND CARRY A *big idea*

A FABLE

THE SEVEN LESSONS TO FINDING
Meaning, Passion and Balance
IN YOUR LIFE AND WORK

DON JONES

WILEY
wiley.com

"The great law of culture:
Let each become all that he was created capable of being."

—*Thomas Carlyle*

"I've gone through life believing in the strength and compe-
tence of others; never in my own.

Now, dazzled, I discovered that my capacities were real.
It was like finding a fortune in the lining of an old coat."

—*Joan Mills*

"Draw your chair up close to the edge of the precipice,
and I'll tell you a story."

—*F. Scott Fitzgerald*

Copyright © 2002 by Don Jones

All rights reserved. No part of this work covered by the copyright herein may be reproduced or used in any form or by any means—graphic, electronic or mechanical—without the prior written permission of the publisher. Any request for photocopying, recording, taping or information storage and retrieval systems of any part of this book shall be directed in writing to CAN-COPY, 1 Yonge Street, Suite 1900, Toronto, Ontario, M5E 1E5.

Care has been taken to trace ownership of copyright material contained in this book. The publishers will gladly receive any information that will enable them to rectify any reference or credit line in subsequent editions.

This publication contains opinions and ideas of the author. They are not presented to provide a basis of action for any particular circumstances without consideration by a competent professional. The author and publisher expressly disclaim any liability or loss, or risk, personal or otherwise which is incurred as a consequence, direct or indirect of the use or application of the contents of this book.

John Wiley & Sons Canada Ltd
22 Worcester Road
Etobicoke, Ontario
M9W 1L1

National Library of Canada Cataloguing in Publication

Jones, Don, 1957–
    Walk softly and carry a big idea : a fable : the seven lessons to finding meaning, passion and balance in your life and work / Don Jones.

ISBN 0-470-83198-7

    1. Success in business. 2. Management. 3. Work and family.
4. Self-actualization (Psychology) I. Title.

HF5386.J778 2002   650.1   C2002-903676-3

Production Credits
Cover & interior text design: Interrobang Graphic Design Inc.
Printer: Tri-Graphic Printing Ltd.

Printed in Canada
10 9 8 7 6 5 4 3 2 1

About the Author

Don Jones is an internationally respected thought leader, speaker, entrepreneur and author whose insights, ideas and overwhelmingly powerful, creative, interactive learning designs have helped hundreds of companies, and over one hundred-thousand employees globally, to align around, and connect to, simple truths and clear ideas they can use to move themselves, their teams and their companies forward.

He has often been referred to as one of the best and most creative designers of business learning experiences in the world today.

In 1988, Don Jones founded exper!ence it inc. (www.experienceitonline.com) with a belief that we are on the cusp of a great era in education; and that corporations will be on the leading edge of the change in the way we look at and experience learning. His globally recognized programs and custom designed classes and experiences continue to push the envelope around what is possible within 'the four walls of a classroom' and beyond. The work of he and his team continues to inspire, amaze, astonish, and ensure that participants emotionally engage with, and are intellectually challenged by specific and profound learning outcomes, rather then being passive receptacles of lifeless information.

The clients who call on Don Jones and exper!ence it inc. are looking for a trusted partner who can help them create memorable, impact-rich, inspirational learning that shifts attitudes, increases skills and knowledge, changes cultures and engages their employees in productive and focused results. exper!ence it inc. has clients and partners around the world from New York to San Francisco, from Tokyo to Chicago and from Istanbul to Toronto, and his programs are now offered in many languages.

Call exper!ence it inc. for more information on speaking engagements or partnering with you to create a change in your team, division, national or global organization; or visit the e! website for more information on the programs and custom services e! offers companies and conferences including the management program *Walk Softly*.

Worldwide 1 (416) 699-6107; N.A. Toll Free 1 (866) 699-6107

email: don@experienceitonline.com
Web site: www.experienceitonline.com

Don Jones lives and works in the Toronto community known as the Beach, the setting for *Walk Softly*. He is the father of Becky and Emma and married to Margot Clayton Jones. He loves to hide treasure down at the beach and have his young daughters *accidentally* find the pirate's treasure map, to travel and explore landscapes and ideas, to collaborate with a great team, to read, write and create. He would work at two things in the world for free: design great, inspiring, hopeful learning environments; and write stories that move people; he is fortunate to be making a living at both.

Contents

Preface

This story is about you and me, about the profound personal and professional challenges we face on the job and at home. On the job we face the challenge of managing and leading first ourselves and then others; at home we face the challenge of giving of ourselves for the benefit of those we love. And it is about balancing the two. It's about the soft skills that make the hard differences. It's the story of one person's movement from chaos to clarity, from isolation to connection, from fear to courage and ultimately toward meaning. It's also a story about Replico Inc. and the *Hook* Theme Park, about pirates and imagination and seeing through a child's eyes again, and about letting another side of ourselves help guide us. Ultimately it's a story about finding within ourselves the unique gifts and talents that we possess and were meant to find and bring forth for those we work with, lead and love.

Walk Softly and Carry a Big Idea was originally written as part of an intensely interactive, classroom-based, simulation program our company designed to help teach the skills behind the challenges of management and leadership at the wonderful, truly world-class Boeing Leadership Centre in St. Louis. It ended up with this publisher because of the overwhelmingly positive response we had from employees within this global company. Some would say, "I am not a reader but I couldn't put this down." Others would say, "This was about me personally, as I am struggling with many of the work and life issues that Scott is." Still other 20 year veterans (business men and women, engineers, scientists, managers) would tell me that they shed a tear in their rooms the night before class, recognizing themselves, their jobs and their family relationships in the story. The debriefing of the book was a powerful classroom experience. Ultimately the hopeful lessons that Eric, the strange and wise janitor, shares with Scott are beacons each reader knew within their heart to be as important to their work as to their life. Each of these seven 'beacons' calls the reader to look at their work and life experience through a new lens; to seek out the positive answers they can and will find within themselves. Inside those answers lies a work and life path of noble purpose, balance, passion and meaning.

Acknowledgments

Being part of a large, eclectic, wonderfully supportive family has always given me a first-hand view of the unique paths we are each meant to walk and the unique contributions we are each meant to pursue, practice and provide. This has given me the courage to follow my own heart; which, more than anything else, has led me to experience it inc., and to finding this story within me. So thank you Cheryl, Patsy, Jeannie, Hal, Val, Greg, Dad and Mom. Mom your love, strength and faith are gifts I can only repay by trying to live up to them—I am blessed. My own growing family has only reminded me about how important those enduring lessons will always be; and this book is for Becky, Emma and my incredibly supportive wife, partner and best friend, Margot.

The second most important job in life to me, besides raising your own family well, is teaching or coaching children in the first years of their life. At this writing I am 45, a husband, father, friend, entrepreneur and author and I still remember my second grade teacher Nancy Hanrahan, at St. Agnes School in Halifax, and her extra efforts with a shy, skinny, red-headed, slightly dyslexic, young boy. You made, and continue to make, a tremendous difference to me, and many others I am sure. Being kind is so often not understood for the genius that it is.

I also want to thank those that have made this story better by their varied and many contributions along the way including Carol Yamada, at the Boeing Leadership Center, a leader I would "step into the fire with" any day; and a number of editors and proof-readers including Rebecca Crichton, Nancy Gall, Natasha Wright, and my editors at John Wiley and Sons especially Karen Milner who supported me from our first meeting—thank you. The work by Marcus Buckingham and Curt Coffman in their book, *First, Break All the Rules*, (Simon & Schuster, 1999) inspired the specific use of the important word 'talent' in this story. Eric Oksendahl inspired the Eric in this story by his wisdom and fun. Jay Howell moved the lesson on meaning forward through our daily explorations of what we both find incredibly exciting and relevant about learning and life. Ron Christian's wonderful work and support of the business has allowed me to grow in many ways of which this book is only one. Thank you all and many more. Your ideas, inspiration and help along the way are very much appreciated.

Don Jones

part one

Soft is Hard

"In the name of God,

stop a moment,

cease your work,

look around you…"

—*Leo Tolstoy*

chapter one

The Beach

"Our prayers are answered not when we are given what we
ask, but when we are challenged to be what we can be."
—*Morris Aldere*

The clear azure sky blended into white just as it touched
the horizon. The April setting sun cast its golden bridge
across the vast glistening lake where Scott stood, feet
fixed, body weighted to the swaying dock, his soul lifted with
each of the water's gentle encouragements. For only a moment,
the kind that lasts a lifetime, he almost lost himself in the grace-
ful movement and stepped courageously across the shiny
bridge to a place of his dreams. But he didn't. Something would-
n't let him. Perhaps the boats caught his eye. They were pulling
out from Ashbridge's Bay, the colorful spinnakers of the
evening's racers cupped the wind, like dancing autumn leaves
at once floating on the ocean and leaping with the wind.

It had only been 10 months since Scott had moved his
family to the beach community in Toronto, twelve months since
he accepted the position within Replico, and eighteen months,

almost to the day, that he had decided he was ready to take on a managerial challenge. Now that he had it, he wasn't sure he wanted it.

There was no hint of the wind near shore as he turned suddenly, as if catching himself doing something he shouldn't, and walked back up the dock to the white and red lifeguard station, the landmark that the old time residents, the Beachers, were fighting to protect. He jumped down to the sand and strolled up and onto the wide boardwalk, heading toward home. Buried in thought, the clear bright colors outside cast in relief the gray din he felt within. Like the wind on the water he thought, all was quiet and beautiful around him, but a storm was whipping itself into a frenzy inside his head.

"There are no pirates down at the beach, Jim! I've told you that a thousand times."

"But Dad, I saw them again today and they buried some treasure down near the lifeguard station. I heard them talk..." The word trailed off, and he stammered and then lost the end of the thought, almost forgetting what it was he was going to say, as if losing a small bright piece of himself. A little glistening formed at the corner of his eye. Too small for any grown up to see, unless they looked very closely. None did. Even at six years old the pattern had already been stored and highlighted in his growing memory. There *were* pirates at the beach, big scary ones, with long, curly, black hair and eye patches, and the biggest pirate, the one with the scar just below his left ear, had a parrot on his shoulder. It would squawk and stare at Jim as he hid behind a bench so he could listen to the pirates tell tales about how many men they had sent to Davy Jones' Locker and how much booty they had hidden beneath the beach—right here in Toronto.

Somehow even at six years old, Jim knew these conversations were not really about whether there were pirates or not; they were only about whether they would be happy or sad in the house tonight. Tonight would be sad, Jim knew. The yelling went on behind him. It wasn't that he couldn't hear the words; sometimes they would poke through the cloud that formed in his brain—short sentences, words that Dad yelled at Mom or Mom yelled at Dad. But usually he heard.

"For God's sake, Scott, he's only six years old."

Mostly the words just got muffled. It was as if he had a filter that sifted and sorted and wouldn't let the bad words come in. Jim would drift out...

"Well, he should be working on his math. He only finished six out of thirty on that Math Minute the teacher has them do every day. Frank's son is up to twenty-four!"

Jim felt himself drift out to a safer place, away from the yelling, far away from their brand new house in Toronto. He could get very far away sometimes, to a world where his pirate friends and foes lived, fought and buried treasure for him to discover. This was a world of mystery, fun, and laughter and more chocolate gold coins than you could ever carry. He could filter out some of their words. And that helped.

"Twenty four!"

But the sadness even crept into this private world too. It was getting harder and harder to fight the dark-haired pirates.
Jim walked out of the kitchen and up the stairs.

"Replico. The pressure is intense, Sabrina. I've got to get out of there!"

"You've just started. You wanted to be a manager. You can't quit."

Scott pulled into the parking lot. His head hurt. It usually hurt in the morning before he got his cup of coffee. Not enough sleep. Too much pressure. Nothing seemed to fit lately. He thought the move to Toronto was going to solve everything. Finally he would have family in the neighborhood. That would ease the pressure at home, he thought. Finally he would get his opportunity to be on the management side of the company. The first rung on a new ladder. That would open the door for a great future for him and let him use the planning and financial skills he had developed. It all seemed to be coming together only a few short months ago, so why did it now seem as if it were all falling apart?

More and more his life was consumed by work. It wasn't that he was always at his desk, but he was consistently putting in fifty-five to sixty hours a week. This started as an interim strategy for getting on top of the job. He was going to get organized and then cut back to around forty-five hours a week. But he never got organized and the hours kept increasing.

He and Sabrina could take this schedule for a while. They had talked about it and she supported his need to get a good start in this new position. Sabrina was incredible. He knew she was ready and willing to shoulder more of the load at home, on top of her work, so that he could find a way to get ahead. Their goal was for Sabrina to take a few years off with the kids, but Scott knew that he needed a more secure footing in management before they could afford both Toronto housing prices and living on one salary. They never thought they would do this; they both expected Sabrina to work right through to retirement. But things had changed and they both had come to the same conclusion a while ago. They would have a second child, a girl this time they hoped, and this time, if they could afford it, Sabrina would take a few years off to care for her.

But the stress on Sabrina and Scott, since they had moved to Toronto, had been tremendous and neither of them was really ready for the challenges that the move had brought. It wasn't just the hours that Scott put in at the office. It was the hours that the office put in at his home. He never left work. When he packed up his desk at night he would always bring a thick portfolio home with him. He almost never opened it. He prided himself on that. But he brought it home anyway. He didn't have to open it. It sat, in all its glorious mess, smack in the middle of his equally messy brain. He couldn't eat dinner, water the small patch of green that he and their neighbors called a lawn, or listen to Sabrina without the contents of that folder spilling out and dancing around his brain. He knew that he couldn't play with Jim anymore without it interrupting him.

He faked it now. He was sure that neither Jim nor Sabrina could tell. He faked enjoying playing with his own son. Faked that he cared what color Jim chose to finish the drawing. Faked that he loved the way that Jim always slurred his r's. (In fact it worried him.) Faked that he noticed that Jim just got a new haircut. "Of course, I noticed. And what a great cut." It wasn't that Scott didn't want to love doing those things, of course he did, it just seemed as if he had forgotten how. Now he knew how to be agitated. That was something that he had really gotten the hang of lately.

Scott slammed the door to his car and walked toward the back entrance to Replico Inc. It was a dingy entrance, just an old metal door with a red spray-painted letter "R" leading to a cement walkway. It could have been any warehouse, anywhere. He didn't like using the front entrance. It was cleaner and fancier and their customers used it, but Scott didn't. But it was too far away from his desk and he always got pulled into conversations that kept him from getting to the pile of work that was waiting for him. Don't these people ever get any work done, Scott wondered. Sometimes while talking with his co-workers, he would make mental notes about the relative degree of competition that he would face as he began his climb up the ladder of his eventual success. He didn't see any stellar competition, a small consolation when he realized that this was the team that his company was relying on to change the direction of the company.

Scott took the two corners, going wide and angling around them like a race car driver trying, each day, to find the perfect angle, the one route that would be the closest to a straight line as possible between his car and his desk, without compromising speed. It was the first part of the day that he enjoyed, this small game meant to increase his efficiency. Occasionally someone would get in the way and he would have to detour around them. This irritated Scott and would throw him off his entire course. He would brush them off and get back on track, but it was never the same.

There was something about the perfection of a straight line that appealed to Scott. It was more than the efficiency that it represented in getting from here to there, although that definitely was a big part of its appeal. There was something almost comforting in it, as if the simple perfection of something as uncomplicated and one-dimensional as a line, a straight and narrow line, could provide a shelter from the inevitable curves that real life would throw at him. Scott loved to plan, to sit down behind the orderly surface of his big brown desk, close his door and shut out the noise and calculate the fastest route from here to there. With great care he would plot out who, what, when, where, why and how for taking both his people and projects forward. It would take him a long time to think of every alternative, every angle, every potential improbable challenge, but in the end he would create the perfect plan. At least it would seem so at the time—the straightest line. He often felt his whole life was a series of lines, straight lines from here to the perfect, continually elusive and always distant, there.

chapter two

The Long Straight Line

"In the long run a short cut seldom is."
—*Malcom Forbes*

The light was just beginning to peek through Scott's window. He was almost the first one in the building today. Monty in shipping was in first. He was always in first, Scott thought. As he tightly cornered the entrance toward his desk he realized that the line from his car to his desk was probably the straightest it had ever been. No one had sidetracked him or made him detour in the slightest. He knew Monty was in, because he'd seen his car out back, but luckily he didn't see Scott. It took him less than two minutes from closing his car door to sitting behind his desk. Precisely one minute and fifty-two seconds; he'd waited to close his car door until the second hand had hit the twelve so it was easy to see. A smile slid across his face. He knew that this was a silly game to play every morning, but he was allowed his own private indulgences. Comforting, he thought. It was going to be a great day. Scott could tell.

Within minutes he was immersed in the details of the meeting that was coming up first thing this morning. It was the first in what was going to be a very exciting project for him and the company. Of course, "exciting" always had a double edge to it. Ching, the Operations and Fabrication manager that he would be working with this morning, had once told him the interpretation for the Chinese characters that made up the word "crisis" could be loosely translated as "opportunity riding a dangerous wind." Scott loved this. That was the way he felt about the company in some ways, though others might not describe the current choices that way. In many ways, that was the way he felt about his career choices as well. He was ready to take the chance and push for change, but he knew that there was a dangerous side to this and that sometime, perhaps inevitably, that wind would work against him. He was ready for that, had planned and prepared for it, he even had a number of straight-line solutions for any and all dangerous winds that would sweep through his projects or try to get in front of his career choices.

Scott almost always felt better about his job when he was doing it. Lately, since he began his new management position, tension always seemed to creep into the rest of his life when he was away too long from his desk. Long weekends were the worst. Both he and Sabrina could sense now when he was starting to get anxious, pensive and ready to get back to whatever challenge he would be carrying with him. Somehow the act of the work itself, the doing of it, sitting behind his desk, signing letters, creating plans, working through the always long checklist that waited for him in the morning gave him great satisfaction, and at the best of times, made him feel like he could do anything.

Scott quickly realized that the skill that had landed him this job and got him noticed above all the other first levels was his ability to focus and get things done. His detailed plans and specific financial calculations impressed his bosses. Long checklists were his strong suit, and he wore them like others wore their cell phones, pagers and Palms. He didn't care for the "efficiency technologies," as he called them. It wasn't that he didn't use them, he did—both his cell phone and pager were always on. He had tried and discarded the Palm, but he found that the most satisfying and practical technology for him had always been a long, handwritten list of "to-do's" with hand-drawn boxes in front of each. Circles in front of the ones where he was waiting for a response. Checkmarks, those wonderfully constructed sets of two connected straight lines, that were becoming an addiction for Scott, beside every completion. He needed to start his day with a cup of the strongest coffee he could find, the straightest line between car and desk he could take, and with as many checkmarks as he could quickly make on his list. Completions, marks against to-do's were to Scott the product of his work—the signs that he was doing something, creating value. If a carpenter could look at the cabinet he had just made with a sigh of satisfaction, if a house builder could hand the owners the keys and see the gleam in their eyes, then a manager, thought Scott, could look admirably at the completed checklists that he hammered and nailed together with his tools. For just a moment he looked around, trying to see if anyone had come in yet. Then Scott quickly opened his drawer and pulled out a stack of long papers. He leafed through them as if he were looking at the animations from a child's flip-book. He lost himself for more than a moment, each sheet with its long list of check-marks, completions, tasks done and value added.

A cool breeze wafted over him, as if he were at the beach. Scott thought it was the flipping papers. Suddenly he heard a noise behind him. It startled him, and he quickly went to tuck the papers back in his drawer, but his fast movements missed their mark and they ended up scattered across the floor, creating a check marked carpet from his desk to the door. Scott suddenly felt embarrassed. He looked up to see a stout, grey-haired man with a small beard that reminded him of King Tut's. The man was standing in the doorway, holding a garbage bag and contemplating the checkmarked carpet. He was wearing loose fitting overalls, crumpled and marked from long wear, a jani-tor, Scott thought, and this soothed Scott as he stooped to pick up his papers with feigned indifference.

"Can I give you a hand?" the man said quietly, as Scott bent to pick up the first of the perfect checkmarked papers. "I can throw them out for you, if you like."

"No thank you. These are," Scott paused briefly, "important papers that I have to keep. But thank you. You can empty my basket though."

"Sure. Glad to." The man went around Scott and started to put the contents of the wastebasket into his garbage bag.

"I've never seen you here before, have I?" asked Scott.

"Oh, I've been around for a while. My name is Eric." And he swiped the side of his big hand against his dirty pants, and extended his hand toward Scott.

There was something in the way he did it that bothered Scott. The way he stood, looked at him, spoke to him and stood over him. It wasn't anything Scott could put his finger on, just a vague, uneasy feeling. Scott stood and put out his own hand, but was still scanning the papers on the floor when he shook Eric's hand. Even as he was doing it Scott knew that he would not be shaking Bob Rabanco's hand, his boss and the Executive Vice President of the Marine Division, in the same hurried way. But this thought, like a puff of smoke in the wind, soon disappeared inside Scott's many calculations, too many and too practiced to even feel like calculations anymore, Scott was always figuring out how to get from "here to the always distant there." He barely noticed as Eric stopped in mid-shake, and before Scott could look up, he was gone. That was rude, just disappearing like that. I suppose that's why he's still a janitor, thought Scott, and he went on gathering his sets of perfectly-connected straight lines and neatly storing them inside the locked bottom drawer of his desk.

Scott wondered what it was about Eric's initial approach that had bothered him. It was something, but he couldn't figure it out and the vague feeling would bounce around inside his head for the rest of the day, surfacing on occasion, but unresolved, would dive below the surface again.

Last night had been better with his son. Jim, thank God, had not brought up the pirates at the beach, and for a change Scott had time to work with him on his Math Minute. The Math Minute was a quiz that Jim's grade one teacher would drill them with every day. Scott liked the routine of this, the expectation of improvement that this particular teacher insisted on and expected from every student. Jim was clearly behind seventy-five percent of the class. Actually out of the twenty students, Jim was usually number sixteen. This was a constant worry to Scott. Occasionally Sabrina would get swept up in this concern as well, but mostly she would just remind Scott how amazingly verbal Jim was, and that he was far and away better at expressing himself than the rest of the class. She said this showed they didn't have anything to worry about. Jim was bright and would learn at his own pace as long as he wasn't made to feel that his own pace was inadequate. That was fine, thought Scott. But the other kids at school were always pretty good at making you feel that the only pace that was adequate was at least average or above. Not too high above, he remembered, but above.

He had taken out a sheet of paper and written out a series of math questions, two plus two, three plus two, five plus four with lines underneath and a space for Jim to write his answer. He would give him one minute to complete as many as he could, and then Scott would correct them. It had gone quite well, Scott thought. They worked together at the kitchen bar, sitting on the tall stools, while Sabrina prepared lunches for the next day. Jann Arden, Scott's favorite singer, played in the background, and, for a change, all had been peaceful and pleasant. The first three times Jim had taken too much time to complete the answers, he would barely get five answers down on the paper. They were always right except the sixes, which would sometimes come out as nines, and the fives as twos. Scott marked these right; with somewhat anxious looks at Sabrina. The teacher had told them that it was not uncommon for this to happen in the early stages of writing and math.

Scott too had problems with a slight dyslexia, which wasn't diagnosed until he was an adult. To this day Scott worked harder on his numbers and presentations than anyone he knew. He prided himself in ensuring that the details of them were beyond criticism. Not so much to excel, although he wanted to; but to absolutely ensure that he wouldn't fail and be humiliated in front of his peers. So when Jim wrote something backwards, Scott was often seeing the little boy sitting next to him with his wavy brown hair and large brown soft eyes, as himself, walking to school ready to be humiliated again.

On the last two of the five Math Minutes they did together Scott started to order the challenges to naturally build on one another. Five plus one, one plus five, five plus two. Jim got eight right this time and burst out with a "Yaaahhhhh!" so heartfelt that Scott almost wept. That joy, that outspoken exuberance, came directly from his mother. Sabrina had a love of life that was natural and never held in check. It was what drew Scott to her from the first moment they met. Unlike Scott, Jim never had a problem expressing and understanding his feelings. Even when Jim was a toddler learning to speak, Scott would say something like, "Jimmie feeling mad?" And little Jimmie, would reply, rarely mispronouncing a word, even from the start, "Actually, just a little sad." Jim's pinpoint accuracy about his own feelings continued and grew. It would sometimes startle guests, and still amazed Scott, who never could get an accurate reading on his own feelings.

It was a nice night; one of the few since they had come to the Beach in Toronto and since he had started his job at Replico. Scott knew there had been too few such nights, but he would make up for it as soon as he could get the ton of stuff off his desk and get to the bottom of the checklist running his life.

He sat in his chair, rhythmically knocking his foot against his desk, deep in thought. The unexplained departure of one of his top people was really bothering him. When he had took over the team, everyone had said that Jessie was the most talented member of his team, but she didn't like to be told what to do. They were right about at least half of it, Scott thought to himself. The previous manager had been far too lax, and Jessie had gotten away with really poor procedures despite delivering usually exceptional results. She hadn't been broken in, Scott knew. She was a wild horse that couldn't be used in a race if your life depended on her. She couldn't take the detailed direction and discipline that he worked very hard to provide, and she wasn't able to sustain the level of production she had the previous year. Without giving reasonable notice Jessie left for another company. We can't match their salaries, Scott thought. If people want just a paycheck, then they can go. Still her departure had upset Rick and John, two of his other team members who had liked and respected her.

Scott walked out of his office and spoke to Joanne, his administrative assistant. "Bob called a cross-functional meeting today; I can't miss that. It's a command performance." In fact he was looking forward to this meeting. It might be just the opportunity for him to get out of his Marketing Department box and do something for the company in a larger way, and to get noticed in the process of doing it. "Tell Mary she has to interview the new hire to replace Jessie. Tell her I'm looking for someone who can walk on water." He laughed as he walked down the hall. Interviewing was never something that Scott spent a lot of time on. It was all a game, he believed. I ask dumb questions and they lie and we both pretend to enjoy it. Not a great use of time for either of us. Scott also believed it showed great confidence in his staff that he trusted them to make the decision.

Scott walked into the meeting and sat opposite the head of the table. It gave him a direct sightline to Bob, who would be chairing the meeting, and allowed him to see every reaction in the room quickly and without turning his head too obviously. This reading was very important to Scott. He likened it to sailors spitting into the wind to check its direction. He rarely reacted to an idea immediately. He never had the confidence to throw his passion behind something right away. It wasn't that he didn't ever want to, he just never felt able to do anything without a lot of forethought and planning. He sometimes felt nervous just asking a question in a group. He was sure that no one would recognize this in him. But he could feel it—surrounding him—some sort of barrier between him and others that affected every minute of every day. It was there, like a sore back—but not noticeable to those around you, but irritating because you knew you were made to walk faster and with more grace.

The others started to pour into the room. Sven from Finance and Business Management came in directly after Scott, followed immediately by Ching. They were deep in conversation and briefly said hello to Scott as they sat down and continued their chat. Maria from Quality Assurance waltzed in and sat beside Scott, and asked how he was doing. They talked for a while, mostly about non-work related issues. Scott had a problem with people from the Quality Assurance Department in general. It wasn't anything personal with Maria, but the idea of QA being a separate arm of the company just didn't make sense to him. If quality was being built in and checked at every stage of the development, then Maria and her growing horde of QA experts were not going to make a difference when the product showed up in her department. He wasn't sure exactly how they did their job, but as they talked, Scott was imagining a radar detector at the airport and the Replico products being passed through it after design, development, and assembly. Then just before they were ready to take off, Maria would swoop down, QA stamped on her Superwoman costume and say, "Sorry, but we have a problem. This ship has a slight break in its mast. Back it goes." Thanks Maria, he said in his head. Just-in-time quality assurance. You just cost the company about ten million bucks by not giving us the money to build better systems. Instead you've been building your QA empire with all of those external consultants I've heard you've been hiring.

"That's what I think we should do. Do you agree, Scott?" Her last sentence interrupted his thoughts and he recovered quickly from the Superwoman costume image and blurted,

"Yes. As long as it makes sense to the group." He thought that should cover him no matter what the suggestion.

"Great. Thanks for your support."

What support? Scott wondered, and he noticed that others had come in while he had been daydreaming.

Jacob from Computers had joined the team and Jameela from Engineering had come in. Bob and Monty were just entering now and were talking about the late shipping problems from last week. Scott could tell. They agreed to meet later on. As Bob sat in the chair opposite Scott, he met Scott's eyes first. Scott nodded and opened his agenda. He had brought today's checklist and also yesterday's. He liked to leave it open, showing a long list of perfect checks, streaming down one full page.

Bob started the meeting and began with a description of the changes that would have to take place in the company. It surprised Scott when Bob actually used the word "crisis," but went on to say that this was not one. To Scott, a denial of something that no one was pressing you on was the same as an admission. Scott remembered Ching's phrase for crisis—opportunity riding a dangerous wind—and caught Ching's knowing eye when the words were spoken. Bob told them that they were the cross-functional team hand-picked by him to take on the most ambitious project the company had ever undertaken. They had the opportunity to win the job for the design and development of *Hook*, the pirate theme park that Spielberg and company had tendered. While Replico was not in the theme park business, they had supplied replicas to most major exhibits in the world. They had never before offered an integrated package of products and services that could sustain a section or attraction at a theme park. This was their opportunity to do just that, Bob believed. Scott noted this conviction on his pad and underlined it: Replico had the skills and talents required but it would take the talents of this cross-functional team to make that potential come to life for the client.

Jacob asked a question but Bob, quickly but not rudely, cut him off. Bob clearly wanted to make a few more points before opening the floor for questions. Jacob seemed subdued after what he likely felt was a dismissal of sorts. Scott noted this, not on his notepad but in his head, as he realized that the reaction to Jacob's next question or suggestion might indicate whether Jacob would have any leverage in moving ideas forward. Scott remembered only too well how at his previous job he had lost credibility early in meetings and was never able to fully recover. This was not fair, he realized, and it happened to people all the time.

Bob wanted to stress that the time for change had arrived at Replico's Marine Division and that anyone who couldn't see that was part of the problem, not the solution. "While the quality of our products is exceptional," Bob said, as Maria sat up in her chair, "the bottom is falling out of the hobby market." They had known for a while that they must expand into other market segments, not only to thrive but just to survive. This surprised Scott, not the actual words but the new intensity with which they were delivered. Competition was heating up in all world markets from global competitors. The facilities supporting Replico's product design, development and distribution were no longer cutting edge. Many others had caught up and surpassed this traditional leader. The brand was suffering, and whether as a result or as a cause, Bob wasn't sure, the employees had never been as dissatisfied as they were at the moment.

Bob believed they could turn this ship around. He had been on board for a long time and had weathered many storms and this ship was not going to stop sailing because of current forecasts. Scott was already growing weary of Bob's constant sea metaphors. A few eyes rolled discreetly. Bob was uniformly respected and liked. He was a decent man and a very capable leader. He treated the staff well, through good times and bad, and helped to build the company to be a world-class leader. People generally trusted him, including Scott, but if Scott heard one more reference to stormy weather, clear blue skies, ship-shape, cast-offs, clean decks, compasses or the North Star, he thought he might be seasick.

The shareholders were pushing for higher returns and the markets were starting to downgrade their ratings of the company. It wasn't a disaster, Bob went on, but the company was at a point of crosswinds and had to decide how it was going to tack. Scott squirmed in his seat and watched the reaction around the table. Aside from the sea metaphors, people were reacting with honest apprehension. They knew the *Hook* theme park represented a rare opportunity, to reposition themselves with a long-time and happy client and make a break into a new future. While the *Hook* people knew them, they were not sold on Replico's ability to make this transition without learning at their expense, and many competitors could boast more experience in tying all aspects of a themed experience together. This was a great opportunity, and the weight on the shoulders of this team would be tremendous.

Scott wasn't surprised when Jacob was the first to ask a question. "Is the company ready to make an investment in the IT infrastructure to support this effort, Bob?"

Bob was genuine in his response but also noncommittal. "We are ready to support a proposal that will win this business and be able to deliver the product cost effectively, Jacob. I saw your last set of requirements and needs, and I have to say that while it was thorough, it needed more substantive support from a marketing perspective."

Jacob was about to say something else when Maria jumped in. "Bob, we need to work on a process that will guarantee that the end product will be delivered on time and to spec. We can't have the issues coming up that have been happening lately in shipping." Everyone in the room understood the implications of her comment. Jacob's shipping computer software fiasco and Monty's latest shipping problems immediately came to mind. Scott admired the efficiency of Maria's message, but moved imperceptibly away from the messenger. Monty's had been around so long that neither Maria nor any new issue was going to displace the relationship that he had with the boss. It was wondrous to Scott. How could someone who was supposed to head up the Quality Assurance situation walk through the "latest fiasco" without feeling the sting, as if shipping times were not part of her responsibility? It was what Scott liked least about the QA role. It gave her lots of ways to interfere but no way to pin any blame on her for anything. Authority without responsibility or accountability. Great job if you can get it, he thought. I wonder what Maria's paid? If it's as much as me, I need to renegotiate.

Bob nodded and looked around the room slowly, watching how people were reacting to Maria. Jameela stammered. She was nervous, and despite her difficulty in expressing ideas she was nonetheless much admired. She started to stammer slightly as she gripped the table with her right hand and said that her team had already prepared drawings and creative directions for the attractions, and that she could share them with the team at the next meeting. Everyone was glad to hear this. Jameela was doing what she did best—her job. Scott respected Jameela. He wondered why she was so nervous; unlike him, her nerves were obvious. Scott always found that her ideas were not only better than most; she and her team moved their ideas forward, not just talked about them. Jameela's nervous voice could sway the group.

Ching joined in quickly. "We have started to look at Jameela's drawings and it's clear that while the fabrication challenges are high, they are within the skill set of our company and with an investment of some resources—not a lot," he threw in hurriedly, "we can create most of the ideas."

"Cost-effectively?" Sven asked. His question was direct and not meant to cut off Ching. They had a long relationship, and this was just another conversation between these two. Neither played politics and neither tried to impress in meetings.

"We can't say that with any degree of certainty until we spec out the jobs more completely. Marketing needs to tell us the size of the investment we can support."

They looked at Scott, who didn't respond immediately. He had trained himself to pause, to think, to never react with direct emotion or with a top-of-mind comment. He pretended to occupy himself for a moment picking up his pen. Most would assume he was coolly taking his time. In reality, his nerves had jumped up a notch and he tried to ready himself for his first comments. "I think Jameela's plans have some merit. I want to ensure, as Maria does, that we can exceed the expectations of our client, and I want to explore more directly with the client how our systems—not just marketing—but our larger systems will affect our relationship with them. I think if we take a strategic approach that communicates our integrated systems to the client, we have a better chance of winning the job. Just as important," Scott knew Bob would love this, "... is ensuring we deliver the same high standard that the world has come to expect from us in our historical business." Just as important. As soon as the words were out of his mouth, Scott wondered whether he had overstated his case. He wanted to ensure that everything that they did would be vetted by the client, and likely through him. It made sense to him, and he wondered whether it would make sense to the others as well.

The group was silent for a moment. They could tell where Scott's comment was coming from. Bob knew it as well. Scott wanted to lead. He didn't want to be a player on this cross-functional team; he wanted to lead it, to take himself and the company forward in one leap. Scott thought about it as one small step for the company, one giant step for his career. He really wanted to take it on. But he also wondered whether others would resent him for it and question whether he was ready for it. Scott was determined not to break the silence first. He looked down as he slipped his pen back into a small pocket on the side of his notepad.

Bob broke the silence. "I agree. If we can get that kind of alignment from everyone, then I think we can win the job and get this ship launched. What do you all think?"

Monty was clearly amused, which confused and angered Scott. Even more confusing was that Monty replied first. "I agree, Bob. Why don't we let Scott use his client contact to guide the team in its new direction? We can work back from the details that Scott's able to uncover."

This made Scott squirm. He had wanted the opportunity, and here was the most experienced voice around the table finding it amusing that he was going to now shoulder the responsibility for leading the team in the transition. Monty was giving him rope and Scott knew, as Monty did, that Scott might end up hanging from it.

Everyone seemed to go along with this, although it was Jameela who seemed the most reluctant. She didn't say anything directly, but for the rest of the meeting she was cool in her responses to his suggestions. Nothing overt, just a feeling Scott got when he looked directly at her. She didn't hold his stare for more than a fleeting instant and then fiddled with her notebook and looked away. It wasn't her natural nervousness, he convinced himself, and he made a mental note to seek her out after the meeting.

The meeting centered around details after that. The discussion went on a circuitous route that covered theme-park attendance, cost of materials, expectations of cyber involvement, safety and insurance considerations. They had, for the interim, at least, a person who was going to have to lead this thing. Scott knew that unless he messed up, he had a great shot at seeing this all the way through as the team head. Scott was sure many in the room were both simultaneously relieved and bothered that he was given this role so casually and so quickly before they even had time to think. He understood that; he would feel the same way if someone else had taken the chance. But no one had. He also understood, as his yellow notepad filled up with a longer and longer list of items, that he was both excited and overwhelmed at the thought of what he had, in just a moment's thought, taken on. He wasn't going to enjoy the conversation with Sabrina tonight about the wonderful trust that Bob and the team had in him. She would immediately see past his presentation and understand that he just put more on his plate than he could bear, because that was the way that he was. She would wonder aloud how in the world he was going to do it, given that he could barely do his "day" job with the hours he was putting in. "There have to be limits, Scott, to what you will take on. What about Jim? Where is he on the priority list?"

"Scott. Scott. You tuned out, buddy." It was Ching, bringing him gently back to the meeting. Scott was embarrassed and started to make an excuse that he was considering some interesting options, but Ching gently said, "Scott, it's okay; we just wanted to know when the next meeting will be."

"Oh. I was just wondering if I would be able to meet with our client's team of creatives next week, or the week after. I think we should listen to them before we start on our plans." Scott felt himself blushing. It started at the collar and worked its way up his neck and the underside of his chin when he was embarrassed.

"Agreed," said Sven. "Perhaps Jameela and Ching and I can take a look at the early concepts and scope them out in the interim."

Heads turned toward Scott. Scott noticed and said quietly, "That's a good idea." Monty's mouth was slightly upturned. Scott was sure he was bemused by the play that was happening in front of him. Scott assumed he had seen it a hundred times before, but not with me as the lead actor, Scott thought. Mission accomplished, he said to himself as they streamed out the door. Jameela was long gone by the time he emerged so he added meeting with her to his list of items to follow up on.

Scott's list was long and he felt apprehensive about that, but he was young, with lots of energy. Sabrina would understand. We agreed that the transition to the company was going to be all-consuming for awhile.

Scott returned to his office and sat in his chair, gently rocking to and fro, blankly staring at the wall, wondering where to begin. Such a long list, so many people to please and so many projects on his plate. He felt overwhelmed. For some reason he remembered the janitor standing over him as he collected his pile of neatly prepared lists. He suddenly realized why he had been bothered by his approach and handshake. It was clear to him now. Eric was more confident than he was.

Scott worked late into the evening. When he called Sabrina, she congratulated him on his new role. She could see it was a good opportunity for him. But Scott heard a hollowness behind her words that wasn't there when he first got the job. They both felt it, but neither wanted to talk about it. It was like walking on a loose board on your deck—you could hear it creak and moan, you could feel it sag and dip, but acknowledging it, looking directly at it, might mean you have to fix it. You just don't have the energy, so you learn to look away, to hide the problem. You can become quite good at this—hiding things from yourself, and from others, for a time.

Scott heard a rustling in the hall and then Eric appeared in the doorway. He startled Scott. It was as if he just appeared out of nowhere. Scott pretended not to be spooked by him.

"Hi, Scott."

"Hi, Eric." Scott was proud that he remembered his name, and was somewhat surprised as well. He added without thinking, as he often did, "How are you?"

Eric walked in to Scott's office, leaned his broom against the molding of the door, and sat in a chair opposite Scott. "Thanks for asking, Scott. I am doing well. How are you doing?"

Scott was surprised by this. Of course, he had asked Eric how he was doing but he didn't have the time or inclination to really want an answer or to have a discussion. It was pushing nine thirty. He didn't have time to shoot the breeze with the company janitor. "Actually I'm a bit rushed, Eric. I still have a ton on my plate before I can leave." Scott thought this would end the discussion.

Eric settled into the chair. "Why so much on your plate, Scott?"

Scott noticed him getting comfortable and was irritated but resigned to the fact that he had opened this conversation and he didn't want to be rude to Eric again. He had blown the night, Jim would already be in bed; likely Sabrina would have gone to bed as well. What's another five minutes, he thought. Scott put his paper down, sat back in his chair and looked at Eric for a moment. His rumpled green overalls were surprisingly clean. He was around 50 but looked younger, thought Scott. The way he sat there, he looked like he didn't have a care in the world. For only a moment Scott felt a twinge of envy.

"Well, it's complicated." Scott said, searching Eric's face for a sign that he didn't really want any explanations.

"Try me." Eric said without blinking.

Scott started talking. He mentioned that he had his team to manage and that was more than a full-time job and now he had taken on responsibility for a cross-functional team. At first he was checking for signs of confusion or boredom but he found himself talking more and more, feeding off Eric's nods and occasional yes's. Scott went on as if he were talking to a passenger sitting next to him on a plane. Eric listened patiently, occasionally saying, "That sounds challenging." or "How will you deal with that?" Scott tried to censor what he was saying, but his voice felt like a flood bursting through a dam. Scott hadn't been able to talk about his work with anyone. After a long time Scott caught himself.

"Listen, that's more than you need to know about my job, and I don't want to bore you with it." Scott added, "Thanks for asking, though." Scott realized that he truly was thankful for Eric asking.

"No problem, Scott. I'm curious about things. You try to get home as soon as you can," he said as he stood up, picked up the broom and slowly emptied Scott's wastepaper basket.

"Thanks, Eric. I will."

Eric walked out of the office and turned down the hallway just as Scott noticed the paper in the basket. "Eric." Scott moved through the door. "You forgot this paper." Scott pulled the rolled-up scrap paper out of the basket and looked around. Eric was nowhere to be seen.

Scott looked at the paper. It didn't look like one that he had thrown in the basket. This had a different feel and slightly old color, like yellowed parchment. He unfolded the paper, and a chill rolled up his spine as he read the words. They were written in script.

Welcome to management school.

Your experience will be your teacher.

I will be your guide.

Pay attention!

Scott looked from the paper to the empty cubicles, then down both sides of the hall. The office was empty. This must be some sort of joke, he thought. He looked at his watch. He must have talked with Eric for about twenty minutes. He couldn't believe it. He grabbed his jacket from behind his office door. He slipped it on and moved through the door, looking one way and then the other. Eric was gone. Scott crumpled the paper and shoved it into his jacket pocket. The office was completely silent, and he felt a cool breeze sweep over him as he walked briskly out the back door and to his waiting car.

chapter three

Picture This ...

"If I accept you as you are, I will make you worse;
however, if I treat you as though you are what you are capable
of becoming, I will help you become that."
—*Malcom Forbes*

It was the beginning of the third week of April when Scott walked into the offices of the Reel to Real Imagination Company (RRI), the hugely successful and creative theme park company in charge of the *Hook* project, he looked up, way up. Hanging from the rafters were suspended three-dimensional letters, each bobbing and weaving around the rooftop canopy of the interior hallway, only occasionally, as if by luck, forming the message that they were intended to convey. Picture This ... The three dots ran off in a line chasing each other until they then completed an imaginary circle and collided in front of the words they meant to trail. Immediately Scott felt out of his league.

"... to see Mary Binacotti." Scott barely said his name and the receptionist, a young, black male with glasses that looked like they were bought in a woman's fashion boutique asked him to repeat it. "Scott ..." he said and this time his last name trailed off. Finally, he got it out and was directed to the red circular sofa that had one opening and was large enough for the four people currently sitting on the inside of the donut not to have to talk with one another. As the fifth he would make no difference to the social space this very cool piece of furniture was evoking in any of these nervous guests. When a young woman came over to ask if he would like a coffee or some other beverage, Scott was very happy to accept the coffee. He almost said that he would also like a slight glaze over himself and his new friends. But he didn't. He lost the moment, as he lost most such moments. Spontaneity was something that he hadn't cultivated. So he waited. Four men and one woman, all younger than Scott, sitting in a ridiculous red donut, without saying a word to one another. Now this is creative, Scott said to himself, sarcastically. He looked around at the timid four, and wondered if they too felt out of their creative leagues here in Donut World.

Scott had now waited too long, and he was getting impatient. He had flown all the way out to California for this meeting and if Mary Binacotti was going to treat him like this he felt like getting up and taking the first flight home and wishing them luck on the project. He would never in a million donuts actually use that option, but it appealed to him.

The last couple of weeks had been very bad for Scott. Since the meeting and the assignment to lead the team, he had not fared very well. The smile on Monty's face, in retrospect, was starting to seem larger and more exaggerated. He even had a dream about that meeting: as he was making his play to lead the project, and he was taking control of the situation and extending his straight line from here to there, there was Monty. In the dream Monty was dressed as a clown, with full makeup and a fat bright red nose, gesturing as if Scott were a monkey. He was throwing balls at him and the others as Scott talked. Why can't anybody else see what an ass Monty is making of himself, Scott fumed to himself in the dream. But the more he talked, the more exaggerated Monty the Clown's antics became, until he was sitting on Scott's lap playing with his hair. Scott was straining to talk over him. Everyone else continued as if the meeting were going on fine.

Even the memory of that dream made Scott sweat. Why can't I just breeze through these things like everyone else, wondered Scott. Why does a client meeting, after all these years and at my age, still make me nervous? He was lost in self-criticism and didn't notice Mary approaching him.

Sabrina had not been understanding about the project. The night that they actually confronted the issue was not a happy one. She had agreed that this would be a challenging year, but it was already challenging. He didn't need to take on a leadership position on this new project. Why couldn't he be just another player on the team, she asked him. He didn't have a good answer. At first he said that it was important to the company, that the team needed his direction, and that if he didn't step up to the plate, then who would? But his reasons rang hollow to Sabrina, and, after a time, they rang hollow to Scott as well. Was it ego? Why did he constantly put more on his plate than he could handle? But on the other hand, he always managed to pull it off.

"But at what cost?" asked Sabrina.

"What do you mean at what cost?" Scott fired back. "You know that this is the cost of me taking on the position that I have. Of course, it will require some sacrifice on my part, on *our* part. That's part of the cost and I thought we understood that coming in."

"We did, Scott. We understood that we were all going to have to sacrifice to make this transition, but it's been just ten months now and instead of settling in, you're taking on more than ever. How is that going to help anybody?"

Jim walked into the kitchen. They lived so much of their lives in this room. Jim sat on one of the big colorful armchairs that flanked the windows. His small body contrasted against the oversized armchair, making him look smaller than he was. He looked tired and was moving a bit slower than usual.

"He has a fever," Sabrina mentioned. "Are you feeling any better, Jimmie?"

"I'm not hot anymore. I don't want to miss school tomorrow," he answered.

Unlike Scott as a boy, Jim was crushed when he had to miss a day of school. Scott worked hard as a child in school but always loved the days when he couldn't go, for whatever reason. Learning was not, for Scott, a great experience. It was a necessary requirement for getting from here to there, something to be tolerated and checked off his list. He was glad that part of his list was finished. Jim was different. He loved school. He would get into conversations with his teachers, even at this young age, and he approached each day as an adventure; well, almost every day.

Scott went over to Jim and picked him up, sat in the soft cushions of the big chair and pulled him onto his lap. He put his hand across his forehead and just under the thatch of soft brown hair and felt the heat streaming from his little boy's head. "Boy, you are very hot young man." Jim squirmed on his lap, trying in a mock way to get away, but wanting his dad to hold him and not let go. Scott didn't notice; he was already thinking about his upcoming meeting with the Reel to Real Imagination Company. He let Jim go. His son squirmed off Scott and rolled onto his back on the carpet.

"How about a game?" Scott said, catching himself thinking about work. Sabrina could see that he had checked out for a moment. Jim got up and ran to get a game.

"Don't run, Jim! You'll be coughing in a second and it will just irritate your fever. Just walk and relax," Sabrina yelled.

Jim brought back a game of tic-tac-toe that Scott had given him last Christmas. It had a wooden base and four white X's and five black O's that you placed within the cut-out squares. Jim loved to play this game, and Scott usually liked to play it with him. Jim placed his X in the middle. He had learned early that this was the square that gave him the most options. Scott placed his O, avoiding the corners. He wanted Jim to win. They played six games back and forth, each taking a turn going first, with Jim winning five out of six and Scott being appropriately disappointed each time. But Scott knew that something was missing from the games, something that he couldn't put his finger on, but had been there last Christmas when they had first played. For most of the time, while this brilliant little brown-eyed boy was whipping him at X's and O's, while Scott lay on the floor and said "yes" and smiled back at Jim, he was thinking about work. Scott wasn't there.

Scott felt ashamed when he realized that even when his family was together, there were really only two people in the kitchen most of the time. It didn't stop him from obsessing about work; it just added to the pressure he felt.

"Hi. Are you Scott?" Mary was standing outside the donut. She was tall, about five foot eleven, thought Scott. She was young and attractive, and she reminded him of someone but he couldn't place her. Or perhaps it was of sometime, another time in his life, maybe that was it. Either way she had a presence about her, something that came across even before she said word, as if she were lighter than everything in the room.

"Yes. And you're Mary, I assume." Scott's frustration over waiting so long seemed to disappear. Almost.

"Yes. I'm sorry to keep you waiting. I was out at an appointment and I got caught in traffic. I was really looking forward to meeting you. I've heard great things about your company from my colleagues."

Scott remembered that she was new here; she was recently hired from a competing company and had a resume that showed exceptional results, he was told. She looked too young to Scott to live up to the reputation that had preceded her, and he wondered how she was able to pull it off. He was looking forward to getting to know her and her team better.

Mary showed him their building; it was built to impress. She was very clear about the strengths of her new company and made no false efforts at modesty. This was the most creative, innovative, challenging place to work on the face of the planet and it was attracting the best people because of it. Those weren't the exact words she used, but that was the impression she left. Scott enjoyed the tour and loved the energy that Mary had for her work and her company. He knew that no one could present the same enthusiasm and energy at Replico. Why? He knew Bob had done that in the early days, at least he heard that he had, but somewhere the spark had been lost. Replico was a business now, a big business, and it felt heavy with responsibility. Scott felt that weight on his shoulders even now as he watched Mary breeze through the different areas of her company, as if she were dancing around a stage built for her performance. Perhaps the fire, the feeling, is supposed to change as the business gets older and the spark dies out. Perhaps this is supposed to be a start-up energy that sustains the vision, but overtime it's replaced by processes and procedures that are required to sustain the company. Yes, that was it, he was sure of it.

The rest of the meeting Scott spent with Mary and two of her colleagues. It bothered him that no one gave him their business cards when he gave them his, so he couldn't figure out who reported to whom. He assumed Mary was in charge, but during the meeting he couldn't be sure. They discussed the details of the Request for Proposal and the relationship that was required to meet their level of expectations. It would be a demanding project. It would require extreme integration within Replico, and with RRI. He made page after page of notes and action items. It was clear that Mary had a great impression of Replico's production quality and an even higher impression of Replico's creative ability than Scott had. He was amazed at how highly regarded his own company was. He currently didn't feel it. But he could also sense skepticism about Replico's ability to make the transition from making the individual replicas to creating an entire themed experience. That was fair, thought Scott. As he wrote, his own thoughts formed and he realized that RRI was open to a new idea and a fresh approach. But by the end of the meeting he was sure that he had jumped in over his head, that his company had nowhere near the level of execution, that they would need, and that he was going to disappoint both himself and the company.

What the hell have I gotten myself into? thought Scott, as he shook Mary's hand at the end of a their long meeting. "Have a good day, Mary. I'll follow up with notes from our meeting and a process that our team will use for ensuring that our solution exceeds your needs."

Before he walked through the massive oak doorway at the front of the building he turned, and almost too quickly, asked, "I can look this up, but just out of curiosity, how long has RRI been in business?"

"Twenty-four years now, Scott, and Replico?"

"About the same." Scott felt deflated. He got into his cab and headed for the airport. A million thoughts swept through his brain. He perceived his own negativity and began to fight it, thinking logically through the events of the meeting. "RRI likes our ability to deliver on replicas, they trust our company, they believe we are creative," this one stuck for Scott, "and they naturally have a need for us to prove we can make the transition to an integrated themed experience, which many of our competitors will have already done." That wasn't, on the face of it, a bad starting point, thought Scott. So why was he feeling so negative about the meeting? He felt tired all of a sudden and as he sat slouched back in the cab, his head dropped and images and memories pulled in many directions.

chapter four

Hooked!

"No men can act with effect who do not act in concert;
no men can act in concert who do not act with confidence;
no men can act with confidence who are not bound together
with common opinions, common affections and common
interests."
—*Edmund Burke*

All the way home on the plane Scott was anxious and fell into and soon out of a troubled sleep. When awake he would twist and turn, worrying about how he and the cross-functional team were going to approach this project, or about how his own team was going to react to all that was on his plate and soon would be on their plates. He didn't see much creative energy or effort coming from his team members, and he didn't feel that they had the resources required to compete. At the same time, Scott knew the company was not in a position to give him everything he needed or wanted. He worried that Replico simply didn't have the talent to move the *Hook* theme park to the point of an exceptional, interactive and fully integrated experience—or to even win the job.

When he dozed off he dreamt of pirates: the competitors who were expecting to swoop down and win this job; the characters that his company needed to be able to create, even the

pirates that Jim said he saw at the beach. He saw swashbuck-
ling pirates, one after another, pour through his dreams, pillag-
ing and plundering his rest and leaving him feeling as if he were
marooned on a desert island without nearly enough resources
for the task at hand.

He arrived home late Tuesday afternoon after a long and
frustrating wait getting through immigration at Toronto airport.
When Scott walked in the door, Jim ran up to him and grabbed
his legs so hard that he almost knocked him over. "Daddy,
Daddy, I have my first soccer game on Thursday!" There was no
greater feeling in the world for Scott than for Jim or Sabrina to
greet him like that. Nothing compared to it, and he treasured
the all-too-brief moment of a son's focused and expressed love.

"That's Thursday night at six, Scott. Can you make it?" Sabrina
looked first at Scott but motioned for him to look at Jim.

Jim was still holding on tight and was now standing on
Scott's shoes. Scott started walking, with Jim riding on two big
black leather magic carpets, into the kitchen and then plunked
him down on the counter. "Your first soccer game. Of course,"
he paused for a second, "I can make it." Scott would make sure
that he was home in time, at least on that night.

Sabrina came over and hugged Scott from behind and she
held on tight, lying her face flat on the back of his leather jacket, not saying anything. Scott could feel that she was tired and
that she was glad he was home. Jim joined in, and the three of
them held there in what Jim called a family hug. "Good to have
you home, sweetie," Sabrina said. "We missed you, you know."

"I missed both of you." He was already starting to remember his agitated sleep on the plane.

"How did your meeting go?" Scott hadn't had time to call before he left for the airport after the meeting, but Sabrina knew that he was nervous going in.

"The meeting itself went well. They're a very interesting company with more energy than I can imagine. But I'm worried that we're out of our league creatively and possibly technically. We might not have the talent or resources to handle the change in direction we're trying to make. I don't think that we can sell them on our ability to do this job."

"Are you sold that you can deliver?" Sabrina always had a way of getting to the point.

"Actually…" He hesitated, looked at his beautiful son sitting on the tall counter, almost at eye level with him, and saw something that he had seen at RRI. He wasn't sure what to call it exactly, but this made Scott feel even more tired. "No, I'm not sold."

The next day, Wednesday morning, he was in early. The line between Scott's car and desk was as straight as it could be. No one else was in and he had the place to himself. He sat behind his desk and looked at the clock. Five o'clock. He would have two hours before anyone showed up, and three hours before most.

Scott spent the next couple of hours going over the list of things he had learned. What had to go into a report to the cross-functional team, what had to go to his team and what were the things that had to end up on his to-do list? He glanced at his long list and noted the performance meeting with Rick that day. He was only partially prepared. He closed his door so that when people came in to work, they would give him a chance to get to the end of his planning before he met with any of them. As he worked Scott started to feel worse. Usually when he sat down and organized himself, he began to feel better about the projects in front of him. Not this time. The further he went into details, the more he realized how far out his initial thinking had been, and how far away their company was from making this right-hand turn into a new future. The more he exposed the details of his thinking to the light of sequence and logic, the more sweat started to appear on his forehead and the longer the list of tasks grew on his plate. There weren't enough hours in the day, nor enough talent or resources in the company to carry this off, he thought. But they are expecting me to manage this, Scott thought.

He opened his locked drawer to get the performance review that he had partially prepared for the meeting with Rick. This was not going to be an easy discussion. Rick clearly was not able to perform as well as the rest of the team. Lying on top of the papers was the folded piece of parchment that Scott had found the night Eric had disappeared. He had pulled it from his coat pocket the next day after Eric's visit and put it in his drawer. He had meant to ask Joanne about it, but it had slipped his mind. He would find out who was behind that prank later.

Scott spent the next half hour finishing his notes for the meeting with Rick. He always felt good about his preparedness, even when he knew that it was not going to be pleasant; actually, in unpleasant cases being prepared made Scott feel even better.

Scott put his head up. The clock said it was almost nine thirty. He had been working intently for almost four and a half hours, and it seemed that he had only been there about twenty minutes. Where do the hours go, he wondered as he got up and went to the door. "Joanne, can you pull the team in for a meeting tomorrow morning?"

"Sure, Scott. You were in early. How are you this morning?"

He was so absorbed in his work that he didn't hear her question and said, "Thanks Joanne, can you make copies of this for each of the team and get it out to them now?" It drove Scott crazy when information that could have been read beforehand was read in the meeting. He always worked hard to make sure that he was ready. He considered this an attribute of a good manager; it was something that he always checked off on his list of things to do for his team. Scott wasn't sure if it was appreciated; in fact, no one even acknowledged it, but he took great pride in doing this and felt that if he didn't, then someone would notice it for sure.

By the time lunch rolled around Scott needed to stretch his legs and get some fresh air. Sabrina had packed his lunch, so he threw on his coat, and slung his backpack over his shoulder. "I'll be back in forty-five minutes or so, Joanne. Just going to get some air."

"See you then, Scott. Have a nice walk. Do you need anything for your meeting?"

"No, I have everything under control." Scott loved to be able to say that. It wasn't just ego; it was also that he was happy that he didn't have to rely on others and could lighten their load through his commitment. That's what a good manager does, he thought.

Joanne looked up from her desk, and watched Scott as he walked away.

The few times Scott was able to get out for a walk along the beach, he loved it. Replico and his home were on opposite ends of the beach. His house was on the far west end of the beach, in the new development where the Woodbine Racetrack had once been. Tearing down the racetrack had offered developers the opportunity to build the largest group of new houses in downtown Toronto in the last twenty years. It had given Scott and his family a new home in the older, traditional, community of the Beach. At the far east end, Replico had taken over, twenty-six years ago, the city of Toronto's water filtration plant. The architecture had been incredible at the time, a wonderful blend of Art Deco and functionality rare in city planning, especially so given its purpose. But it had been neglected and except for the entrance, which Bob ensured was maintained for clients, the old building had largely lost its appeal and was falling into disrepair.

But it offered employees the beach to stroll at lunch, and for Scott it was a short twenty-five minute walk along the boardwalk from home, although he rarely did this. He preferred to save the time and take the five- to ten-minute drive. He knew he was lucky, as most of his neighbors had forty-five minute commutes across the city, sweating it out in rush-hour traffic.

Today Scott needed to get out. The upcoming meeting, his overfull brain and the tasks ahead of him forced him out of the office. The water and sky were incredibly beautiful. A jigsaw of small, light gray clouds formed and reformed just on top of the horizon. Very few people were out. The Beach area of Toronto during late April didn't have the appeal that the middle of summer did for ninety percent of the city, but increased it for the residents Beachers—who found themselves strolling without crowds on a beautiful boardwalk surrounded by the many shades of blue that make up sky and water, feeling the warmth of the promise of summer on their faces and the sounds of birds and children and open silence filling them full. He recognized a couple of faces as he strolled but didn't say hi. As soon as he had drunk in the fresh cool air and felt it on his cheeks, he wondered why he didn't do this more often. Next year, he thought, when I get out from under the current projects and get this new job under control, I'm going to come down here every day, he promised himself.

He stopped at the Leuty Lifeguard Station and climbed up onto the dock. He was out of the wind as soon as he sat down against its chipped white walls, the dock extending out in front of his outstretched legs and feet. He pulled off his backpack and opened it, took out his sandwich and drink, and pulled out the file he had brought. He sat there, the warming sun penetrating through the cooler spring air, and read and reread the long list of to-do's that he had prepared. He sat there erasing the initials on one line and putting them on another.

"Come on in, Rick. I'm glad we could finally make this meeting happen." Both men had cancelled it twice now, and neither of them was glad to finally be meeting.

Rick didn't comment. "Hi, Scott. How was the meeting in California?" His whole team was on alert about California. They knew this right-angle turn the company was trying to make, could force a one-hundred-and-eighty degree change in their plans and they hadn't heard anything from Scott about it.

"It was a great meeting, Rick." Scott immediately moved on. He didn't like to share information with one employee only; it was a rule with Scott. He would wait for tomorrow's meeting for that. He would give them a pep talk about the opportunity that awaited them. He definitely needed to prepare that, as he didn't want to infect them with his own doubt about the project.

"Rick, I need to talk to you about your performance lately." Scott didn't see the need to waste a lot of time beating around the bush. "I'm very concerned that you don't seem able to work at the same pace as the rest of the team and that your numbers are showing it. Your marketing projects," Scott scanned his list and made a checkmark, "show that your products are not generating the numbers we need."

Rick was silent for a while and when he did speak, Scott thought he was defensive. The conversation covered the ground that Scott needed to cover. One by one Scott built his case, proved his points and checkmark after checkmark, made it all but irrefutable. Rick made an effort to move the subject to other areas where there was less concern with his performance, and, while these were valid, Scott was very clear he needed him to improve on his weaknesses. "Rick, if you can improve on these things, we can shore up the team. I need us to be having a different conversation six months from now, and I'm sure that we will."

Rick wasn't pleased with the outcome of the performance review. Scott wasn't pleased to have to deliver the news. But that's part of being a manager, Scott thought, and I took the job knowing that.

Scott's team filed into the room en masse. It looked as if they were just leaving a meeting rather than coming into one. This unnerved Scott. What could they have been meeting about, he wondered. This brought another issue to mind that he had meant to talk to them about but had forgotten. Well, now might be a good time, he realized, and he let his carefully planned presentation of the RRI meeting slip out of his mind for the moment.

"Good to see you all again. I've been extremely busy with my regular job and now with Bob's initiative, it's been crazy. But I wanted to talk to you about a couple of things today."

Scott pulled out his list, although the first item was not on it. "First, I've noticed that we're spending too much time shooting the breeze with one another." He continued, "I'm all for good communication, so don't take this the wrong way, but I've noticed a lot of standing around in each other's cubicles. I've also noticed that we're getting behind in some of our projects. We just don't have time for this."

Everyone was silent. John looked over at Rick. Rick looked down. Toby, the new replacement for Jessie, didn't take his eyes off Scott. Scott had not had time to sit down formally with Toby yet, but he would in the next week or so. Sara was about to say something when Emma broke the silence first and spoke. "Scott, I think that's an overreaction. I haven't noticed any extreme misuse of time on anyone's part, and I get to see just about everything from where I s..."

Scott interrupted her before she could finish. "Don't get me wrong. It's not extreme, but it doesn't have to be. The little things make a big difference, Emma." This would be a good lesson for the new hire, Scott thought. "I learned that back when I was at your level. Those few minutes add up and make a big difference. So all I am asking is that you watch it, that's all. I'm not asking for more." That was reasonable, Scott was sure.

"Secondly," and Scott now got back on his agenda, "I met with RRI, and in my view we can win this thing. We can help the company make a turn from our traditional business to this next level of opportunity—a total integrated themed experiences." He motioned to a paper that he would hand out at the end of the meeting. "I'm going to need one-hundred-and-fifty percent effort from all of you over the next six months or so to pull it off. We've been given a lead position on the company's cross-functional team. Bob wants us to ensure that we align our internal processes and products with the customers' needs. We're in the best position to guide the company."

There were a million questions after that. The anxiety in the room went through the roof. Scott was hoping for a bit more enthusiasm. Where was the entrepreneurial spirit he could taste the moment he walked into RRI? He looked at his team, even as he was answering their questions and was already disappointed in them. He referred many of their questions to the prepared information. The meeting went long past the hour he had planned, and he pensively glanced back and forth between his watch and his to-do list until he finally closed the meeting. No one likes a meeting to go too far over its allotted time; he knew that.

Scott was exhausted. He dragged himself back to his office, closed the door and sat back in his chair. He was tired but he also felt sad and angry. Where the hell is the spirit of this company? No one jumped to take anything off his plate, like he did back when he worked for Ab Larose, his old boss and mentor. Where are the keeners? What happened to initiative? Everyone wants a corner office right out of school, but no one wants to work for it.

The next day, Thursday, just turned a bad week into something much worse. Rick submitted his resignation and offered to give the company four weeks notice, more if they needed it. Scott was stunned, and in his quick reaction said that two weeks would be fine. He wished he hadn't spoken so fast, but maybe it was just as well since Rick was going. It was perhaps best if he left right away rather than infecting the others with a negative attitude. Scott asked him, "Doesn't your new position require you to start at a specific date?" The answer hurt Scott, but he tried to ignore its implications.

"I don't have another position lined up. I talked it over with my wife," he hesitated for a moment, "Tricia." Scott wouldn't have known what her name was and they both knew it, "And we agreed that it was the best thing to do for me and my family at this time."

Scott spent the rest of the day putting out fires, trying to start the process of finding a replacement for Rick, meeting quickly with the new hire, Toby, who seemed technically average at best and ignoring the long silences when he walked into the team's areas—his team was overreacting to his comments about focusing on their work, he was sure, and working late into the evening trying to manage his growing to-do lists.

When everyone was gone, he closed his door and slumped into his chair. He had never felt this overwhelmed before. Scott didn't know what he could or should do. So he did what he always did. Without thinking, he started to make more to-do lists—for himself, for each of his team members, for the cross-functional team. But as he progressed he was just getting more muddled and confused, and for a time he just sat there, staring at the reams of paper strewn across his desk.

Scott was startled to hear a knock at his door. It opened slightly, a breeze wafted in and Eric stuck his head around.

"Just here to clean things up a bit, my friend."

Without thinking, Scott reached under his desk and passed him his wastebasket. Eric emptied it, gave it back to Scott and asked what time it was as he walked out the door.

Scott was placing his basket back when he saw it. In the corner of the basket was a crumpled piece of paper, the same type as last time. He reached in for it, ignoring Eric's question.

He looked at the paper and studied the script, without really taking in the words.

"Eric!" Scott shouted. He wanted to stop him this time and find out what kind of joke this was. He got up from his desk and ran to the door. Scott could see the back door closing and hear the silence of the office once again envelop him. Why would he ask what time it was, Scott asked himself, if he wasn't going to stick around for the answer? Besides he could have just looked at this clock, thought Scott, as he glanced up at the clock on the wall behind him.

Damn! It was eight o'clock. He looked at his watch. "I've missed Jim's soccer game." He felt an intense pain now, right behind his ribs. A constriction. He knew that he had just crossed a line that he didn't want to cross. He had put himself into a situation that he didn't know how to get out of.

He went back to his office and slumped into his chair, the ball of crushed parchment still in his hand. He flattened it out on his desk, smoothing the wrinkles with the sweaty palm of his right hand. This time Scott read it, as if seeing the words for the first time.

Management Lesson Number One

Soft is Hard

Business is not just about numbers,
and life is not just about facts.

Soft skills create hard numbers.
Great managers manage themselves first.
Your future as a manager is through people.
You will learn this through wisdom
or experience.
It is your choice.

Scott crawled into bed much later that night, hours after Sabrina had fallen asleep. Pirates invaded his dreams again and he found himself a captain of a ship's crew competing to find and keep a hidden treasure. Without the resources to keep everyone focused or happy, crew left and mutinied or were abandoned on deserted islands. Scott, a captain was left wondering what he could do to keep his crew under control. Before he fell into this fitful sleep Scott had replayed this evening's welcoming home from Jim. He played it over and over until he couldn't take it any more.

Jim had been up when he got home. Scott knew that he must have been wired after his game; otherwise Sabrina would have had him in bed and asleep long ago. Still Jim enthusiastically greeted his dad. "Dad, Dad, I played my first game." He ran over to him.

Sabrina was furious, Scott could tell without a word being exchanged, and he couldn't blame her. "I know, Jim. I couldn't get out of work in time. I really wanted to be there." He didn't look at Sabrina as he spoke, but focused on the little boy in front of him.

"It's okay, Dad." Jim looked at the ground, his voice trailing a bit. "I didn't score any goals today."

This made Scott's throat swell up and his eyes fill with tears. He grabbed his son and pulled him to him, holding him as close as he ever had.

"That's okay, son," his voice trailed to a whisper. "Neither did I."

part two

*The Journey into
Meaning*

"We are all like one-winged angels.

It's only when we help each other

that we can fly."

—*Luciano deCrescenzo*

chapter five

The Horizon

"The only ones among you who will be really happy are those who will have sought and found how to serve."
—Morris Aldere

S cott was woken by tremors shaking his house. At first he thought he was dreaming but then realized that the house really was shaking. Sabrina was still sleeping, but Scott got up and went to the windows. Down below, workers were starting to dig the foundation for the row of houses that would sprout up and obstruct their view of the beach.

He opened the door to the small balcony and walked out and looked out over the Summerville Olympic Pool, the above-ground structure that housed the three Olympic-size swimming pools and diving tank. He had heard that they had built it above ground because the watery sandy soil would have, over time, destroyed an in-ground pool. From his balcony he could see one corner of one of the pools and the diving structure of another sprouting up into the air high above the level of the pool's surface, very high above the ground. He could see over this to the horizon where lake met sky in a calm celebration. To the right of the pool was the kids' playground, park and trees, and to its left the large expanse of the beach, which curled around the point and hid from view the walking paths and small sailing club behind it.

The view was nice while it lasted, he thought. It had taken the builder a long time to sell the expensive condos that would circle their neighborhood and face the beach directly. But they must have finally sold. The view of the beach would be lost, but he hoped that the view of the water above the tree line and above the Summerville Pool would still be intact. Something about being able to see a horizon appealed to both Scott and Sabrina. It was the same way that he felt about being in the back seat of a car; he had to stretch his neck to ensure that he could see far into the distance. He craved the perspective that distance and time brought, that a horizon provided. He had lost this viewpoint. The urgency and size of his to-do list just wouldn't allow for this longer view, he convinced himself.

"Joanne, can you call Jameela for a meeting here in my office as soon as she is free?" Scott asked as he breezed by her desk, half-surprised and somewhat disappointed that she beat him in this morning. A manager needs to work longer than his staff, Scott believed.

"Good morning, Scott." Joanne said with humor. Scott missed it and kept walking.

"Thanks, Joanne," he said, entering his office and closing the door. Once he was seated and had pulled out his papers from the work that he had brought home the night before, he unlocked his bottom drawer and pulled out the two parchments. He flattened them out and read and reread them. He couldn't figure it out. Why would someone play this trick on him? What would they have to gain? Maybe his team was trying to send a message to him. "Pay Attention!" he read. To what? How did they get the janitor to pull it off? Joanne knocked and walked in. Scott folded the papers with a deliberately casual air, put them back into the drawer and slid it shut.

"Jameela's assistant, Katrina, says she'll be tied up for the next two weeks, but perhaps the week after next would work for her. Is that soon enough for you Scott? If not, Katrina says she can meet with you this week."

Joanne knew it wasn't soon enough. Scott never asked her to book a meeting that he didn't want to happen within the same week. Jameela understood that the cross-functional project was a high priority. For her to put him off for two weeks was unacceptable. Scott was insulted and now knew that something was wrong. This reinforced the icy cool feeling he had sensed from Jameela during the meeting. The fact that she wanted to send her assistant was the icing on the cake. "No, that won't be soon enough, Joanne. I will call her myself." His irritation was evident. Scott hoped that Joanne knew this was directed at Jameela and not at her, but he didn't stop to check.

Joanne didn't respond and went on to another topic. "Do we have the resource plan in place for the RRI project, Scott? If not, I can prepare it for you and we can go over it together." This wasn't her area of experience, only her interest, and they both knew that. She had been hired because she was a good assistant, but she kept trying to move into the project area and involve herself in the details of the plan. That area was his responsibility. If she contributed that would be great, but not at the level she was suggesting. He would have been very surprised if she had even tried anything like that before.

"Thanks, Joanne. I still have to do that; but I'll have it by early next week. Besides, it requires some cross-functional input at my level, and I had better coordinate that. Please review it to see if I missed anything once I put the outline together." That was about as diplomatic as he could get, he thought. She was a good team player and a decent assistant, but she had to improve in a number of areas before he could promote her to the kind of work she was talking about.

"But I think I could do it." She paused. "Very well." It wasn't like Joanne to add adjectives to her own efforts, he thought. She didn't move, just looked at him.

"I'm sure you could take a good crack at it, Joanne. It's just that we have so much on your plate right now. I think you should ensure that you get through those things, complete them at a high level and then we can take look at the type of projects we move onto your list."

She nodded and got up to leave his office when he decided to ask her. He hadn't been sure he would. He made it sound very casual. "Have you ever met Eric? The janitor?" he shuffled some papers to appear nonchalant.

She turned around. He could tell that she wasn't happy but that passed, as it did easily with Joanne, he thought gratefully. "What was the name again?" she asked.

"Eric. He's a night janitor. I see him sometimes when I'm in late at night."

"Actually Scott, I don't think we have a night janitor. We have the building services group who come in during the day, and into our offices just as we leave, and on the weekends I think. No one but security is here late at night. Are you sure he was a janitor and not a repairman or something?"

"Yes, that was likely it, a repairman. Just wondering. He was a pleasant fellow." Scott didn't want to pursue the question further and continued to move paper from one side of his desk to the other, and then back again.

Joanne realized, as she was answering Scott's question, that he hadn't been there for their conversation. She was furious, it was as if his energy had changed and suddenly showed up, but not for her—for himself.

Repairmen don't empty wastebaskets, thought Scott, and he shivered.

Scott dialed Jameela's number.

"Hi, Scott," Katrina must have read his number. "I understand that we'll be working together on the *Hook* project." Scott was shocked. What is Jameela trying to pull? If he wanted to work with an administrative assistant he would have chosen Joanne, but right now he wanted to work with the head of the design and engineering team.

"We'll see how the project develops. Is Jameela there?"

There was a slight pause before she responded. "Sure, Scott. If you want to hold for her, I'll let her know you're on the phone."

"Okay."

About a minute later Katrina came back on the line. "She might be another minute or two, Scott. Would you like her to call you back?"

"Fine." He hung up.

Scott was furious. He had first noticed Jameela's cool reaction in the meeting. Now she'd put off a meeting with him, offered her administrative assistant as a replacement and put him on hold. Who did she think she was—the Queen? He was determined to get to Jameela today. It was a to-do that was high on his checklist, and he wasn't going to let whatever was going on stop him.

He spent the next while waiting for the call. Scott tried to do some work but made no progress he just kept staring at the phone. With every minute that went by, he created one more reason to dislike Jameela.

"Scott," Joanne called, "Jameela is on line one."

Scott wanted to say that he would call her back. But it was no use; he wanted to talk to her more than she wanted to talk to him.

He picked up the phone and sat firmly back in his chair. "Hi, Jameela."

"Hi, Scott. How are you? I wanted to talk to you after the meeting the other day, but I had to run to another one. How was it for you?"

Nice try, he thought. "It was good. I think we can do a great job if we use our resources well," he lied. "What did you think?"

"To tell you the truth, Scott, I don't see it. I was worried, not that Bob won't support the turn in direction, but that something is missing in our ability to compete in that market and win this project."

Scott thought this was a reaction to his leading the team. "You don't think we can pull it off?" he said, defensively.

Jameela didn't react to his tone. "I just wonder, when I look at what we've done and the way we're currently resourced, whether we have the creative ability and the technical support to pull it off and win the thing."

Scott thought she was right, but he didn't feel he could share his doubts so openly with others at work. He felt trapped. He couldn't lead and not believe, but he couldn't be honest either. "We're going to win the contract, Jameela. We can blow the competition away if we get everyone behind it."

"Well, I'm glad you see it that way, Scott. Good for you. So what can I do to support you and the team in this initiative?"

Scott wished that he could share his doubts and talk more about hers. He couldn't. To Scott, leading and managing others required him to show a courageous front when others showed only doubt. He was sure that it was one of the reasons he was given this management opportunity.

"I need us to get together to map out the plan for reviewing how design and engineering will receive and use our customer information for the pitch. I can't wait two weeks for that."

"I think that's exactly what needs to get done, Scott, and I'm glad you are looking at this. I suggest that you and Katrina get together as soon as possible."

"I can't believe you're downloading this to your assistant." Scott couldn't contain his impatience. The pressure just seemed to roll in like a tidal wave with that comment. "This is one of the most important initiatives for our company, and I'm committing my time to it. I need you to as well."

"Scott, I appreciate that and I support it. But Katrina is more than capable to work on the first steps of this with any members of your team," she paused, "including you. She's more than capable in the areas that you need feedback in. She'll bring me into the loop when I'm required. That's her job."

"Well, what is *your* job then?" Scott was almost yelling, and he didn't like it.

She took a deep breath, as if she had seen this coming and wanted to get it over with. "My job is making decisions to hire the right talent, assign to the right level of challenge and then get out of their way." She was not happy about this conversation, and she was making that clear. "I'm sorry you have a different opinion of Katrina's ability, but that's not your call. I make that decision, and you can decide whether you want to meet with her or not."

There was a long pause on both ends of the phone. Scott was fuming and Jameela started talking, this time in a calmer voice, "Listen, Scott. The first meeting needs to spec out needs and determine process. Kat's much better at that than I am. She will determine who on our team will be required for next steps."

Scott was silent. He felt like he was being lectured. This was the first time he didn't hear any nervousness or hesitation in Jameela's voice. "Thank you very much, Jameela." Scott's tone was clear: He was not grateful. "I will have someone from my team follow up with Katrina soon." Even as he said it, he wondered if he could. No one on his team was ready at that level, but he didn't want to admit it. As he hung up, he felt the pressure building in his head, and he didn't see a nice neat to-do forming in his mind's list that would make it go away.

The rest of the day had flowed by since his morning call with Jameela. When he looked up from his desk he realized that the lights in the office had gone off and the track of nightlights had taken their place. He hadn't stopped after the phone call with Jameela. There was no way it was going to be him and Jameela's administrative assistant making the plans to go forward. If someone on his team was going to get the ball rolling with Katrina, then he needed to provide that person with a step-by-step process, ensuring that it would get done right. It was unrealistic for Jameela to expect so much from her staff. Scott prided himself in not doing this to people. He had seen too many bad managers put people in over their heads and then end up taking off their heads for the results. He worked late into the evening ensuring that the tasks for that meeting were documented and that the individual steps for proceeding were tied down. Good management eliminates chaos, thought Scott.

chapter Six

Chaos

"It is a fine thing to have ability,
but the ability to discover ability in others is the true test."
—*Elbert Hubbard*

Scott's car didn't start Monday morning and Sabrina needed the minivan to take Jim to the doctor's for a checkup.

"No problem, sweetie, I'll walk." Scott offered. As he looked out the window on this early May morning, only a few gray clouds clustered together and the rest of the sky looked clear. "Thanks, Scott. Bring an umbrella, though. It looks like rain."

"No, I'll be fine. Bye, Sabrina. Bye, Jim." He was already calculating how he was going to make up the additional fifteen to twenty minutes he would lose because of the walk. Scott realized that he didn't kiss them goodbye in his rush to make up the time.

"Bye, Daddy." Scott could hear his son from the sidewalk, and he turned to see Jim in the window waving at him. Scott thought about running back up the stairs and giving him a hug, but he just didn't have time. He could already feel the rest of the day starting to pour over him like hot oil.

No sooner had he stepped across Lakeshore Boulevard and behind the Summerville Pool than the sky turned from light gray to black. Scott barely noticed; only quickened his pace a bit, heading east along the boardwalk at a rapid clip. The wind picked up and small waves, their tops peaking over with white caps, started to crash on the beach. Only on windy days did waves create any caps at all on the lake. Within minutes, by the time Scott had passed the tennis courts and the outdoor rink, a thunderstorm ripped open the clouds. Big gushes of water poured down and dropped like heavy sacks, stunning people, cementing them in their tracks. Scott finally noticed. The first rush of water stunned him with it's force. It almost hurt.

The rain was so heavy and quick to develop that Scott could barely see the lake. He headed under the overhanging canopy of the ice cream shop just past the rink. He stood there for what seemed like a very long time, getting progressively wetter and colder as the rain slashed at him. After a time, the door of the shop, normally closed until the consistently warmer weather that June would bring, opened behind him and the owner, who must have been cleaning or repairing something, told him to step inside. Scott was grateful for the respite and could feel the heat rolling out the door, even as he was standing outside. He stepped in the door and thanked the bent older man who went back to work behind the counter.

Scott stood in the window, looking out through the blank eyes of an ice cream snowman drawn onto the large picture window. He looked out at the wet cold day, looked down one side of the boardwalk and then the other. Both empty. He watched the waves crash on the beach, each one larger and harder than the one before. He watched the lightning crack over the lake and listened to it explode closer and closer. It sounded like music to him as he counted, as he had done as a child, the time between the light and the sound. He watched the cold wind whipping branches loose; and once free, driving them circuitously to the shoreline where they stuck to the rocks or caught the water lightly only to dance up again with the wind. It was as if the freed branches were graced with a lightness that the world of gravity forgot to include in its heavy tome of rules. Watching this cold gray day crash around him, turning blacker and blacker, Scott felt the store's warmth flow through him and a peace that he hadn't felt in a long time flow along with it. It spread luxuriously inside him rounding hardened edges as it went, settling into him, settling him, and at the same time suddenly making him tired and drained.

Scott realized that he didn't want to go east along the boardwalk. He didn't want to fulfill one more obligation; he didn't feel like he could—not with his own team, not with his cross-functional team, not at Replico, not at all. And he realized, with a weary resignation, that he didn't want to head west either. He didn't want the burden of responsibility that a decent

dad and husband carries well. He couldn't bear to leave anymore worrying over fifteen minutes or missed soccer games.
Where has the joy in my life gone? He was blanketed in obligation, heavy and stifling.

On this churning black day only the eyes of the snowman
remained fixed, heavy, turned down and to the front, neither
looking left nor right; for a moment only, for an impossibly thin
slice of time, something within the snowman died. It didn't
melt, it suffocated.

The wind continued to strike and compel parts of the
earth to move with it. The sound of the storm dominated the
beach. Branches were pulled from large trees, leaves spiraled,
water and sand mixed in a mid-air dance, and everything was
moving, being torn, tossed and twisted. Chaos. Some things
were dying, while others, invisible to Scott, were being born.

The storm passed. As mysteriously and suddenly as it
came, it was gone, leaving behind a wet day, torn branches
strewn across the boardwalk, a now carved-out birch where a
lightning strike had ripped it apart and split off about a third of
it, felling it in the soggy grass. Scott walked home, changed and
then called a cab to take him to Replico.

Once behind his desk Scott was swamped with the urgent. Even
Scott realized that the important longer-view perspectives were
lost behind the constant buzz that vibrated inside his brain.
There was no way to find a horizon. No way to find a calm view

of the world. Everywhere he turned there was only urgency and pressure, a constant building pressure. On his desk were stacks of messages scribbled on note pads, memos and an overfull in-basket with letters and packages for him to sort through. They sat on his desk, each one sending out messages. Perhaps they could contain resignation letters or letters, which, if not answered, would lead to one. When Scott turned on his computer there was a long list of e-mail waiting for responses, every second one asking for an immediate return. His voice mail was full, and he hung up as soon as he heard the number of messages it contained. His pager rang and startled him so much that he jumped from his chair. He didn't pick it up, just stared at it. He was like a shell-shocked war victim cringing at the slightest noise. Each tiny knock could be a bomb. Every message could contain explosive material. He knew it was irrational, and that only made him feel worse.

For a time, amidst everything, with the constant vibrating inside his brain, the pager still ringing, the stacks and memos still ready to attack, he froze. He couldn't move. He wouldn't have been able to talk now if someone had asked him something. He just stared down at the pager, numbing himself to the reality that was encircling him until silence fell around and within him. He stood like this for what seemed like a very long time. He was embarrassed by it. "Get a grip. What the hell are you doing?" one voice said. It was answered quickly and confidently by another. "You are failing, Scott. That is what you are doing. Failing." These voices would not be silenced, and he stood there, feet fixed, body swaying as if on the Leuty dock, while he punished himself for crimes unknown even to him.

The week went on. The voices came and went on their own schedule. He functioned. He sat, stood, walked, talked. He answered e-mails, letters, voice mails and pagers. He met with people and sounded confident when he thought he had to. He ignored the silences and walked through, past, over, under and straight into problems. He worked late and never caught up, and all that time he never once, not once, felt like what he was going to do next was the right thing. Not once during the entire week did he feel that the thing that he just did would make a significant, positive difference to anybody. But still the week went on.

"John, can you bring me up to speed on the how the new project proposal is coming?" That sounded as casual as he could make it.

"Sure, Scott. I'll be right there." John exchanged a knowing glance with Emma, as he reached to pick up the file from his desk and followed Scott into his office.

"Are you finished the project plan for the new marketing campaign?" Scott badly needed this to be finished as soon as possible. How was he going to start to make a dent in the RRI proposal process if he couldn't get the regular work out the door faster than planned? It was the start of the second week of May and things had to start moving forward.

"Well no, Scott." He sounded indignant. "I'm a good three weeks from finishing." Where the hell is that tone coming from, Scott said to himself, but he knew that he didn't want the answer. There was more than just a sense of frustration in John's voice. "I sent you a memo last week. You never replied to it."

I have so much on my plate, John, that you wouldn't have a clue about and wouldn't, I'm sure, care about, Scott yelled inside his head. He could feel himself skipping defensive and moving into aggressive, but he caught himself and managed to utter a controlled, "I've been backed up a bit lately on my memos, John. What did it say?" He felt both angry and humbled at the same time. He knew he had lost any advantage on this discussion and was now at John's mercy.

John opened his file. The memo was printed and on top, as if he had been building his documentation for just such an encounter. Scott sat back and watched the play unfold as John would likely have predicted it would.

"Last Tuesday I sent you an e-mail titled Project Plan Review, Reply Requested and copied the rest of the people on the team and Bob as well." It bothered Scott that the e-mail had gone to Bob. Why? What kind of a game is John trying to play?

John continued, "Our supplier, that you chose last month," that's it, he's going to try to blame the delay on me, Scott fumed to himself, "was delaying us for the third time and I was requesting permission to drop them and go through the selection process again. An abbreviated one this time." He paused for a moment and looked up at Scott. He was neither worried about the implications for the company nor for himself. He just looked at Scott as if to say, "That's just the way it is. Any ideas?" He then went on to finish. "I stated that if I heard back right away, I could complete the turnaround in about two weeks, with the window we had with the supplier. Since I didn't hear back from you, I think the time estimate is about three weeks from now."

"Well, this won't do, John. I expected that this would be almost done by now and you're telling me that we won't be finished for another three weeks. We have stuff rolling at us—we have to clean our plates for this." Scott couldn't contain himself. Everyone was throwing blocks in his way. John sat there and stared at him. He knew he had covered his ass, Scott thought, and he could just stare. For now. "Why didn't you come to see me about this? It's not acceptable to say you sent me a memo."

"Scott, you were the one who said we shouldn't bother you when your door's closed. It hasn't been open for over a week. Joanne said you weren't taking appointments until you cleared your desk."

Scott waited for a moment. "Okay, switch suppliers if you have to."

"It's going to cost us a premium at this point, Scott. You realize that, don't you?"

Scott lost his thin veneer of control and yelled, "Yes, I realize that." Scott's budget this year was through the roof but what choice did he have? John got up and left. Scott felt totally humiliated. He was coming dangerously close to losing it completely. He could feel the pressure building, but as he looked around at the landmines and unexploded mortar shells on his to-do list, he couldn't see anyway out.

Scott got up from his desk and made a flourish of scooping up some papers. He put them in his bag and headed out the door. Joanne was surprised as she didn't think he had any appointments that afternoon. "I just realized that I have an appointment downtown," he told Joanne. "I'll be back around 4:30 and work into the evening, so I'll get you that document for you to process tomorrow morning."

She didn't look convinced. He walked out the door and ducked into his car, the shop had dropped it off during the day, and drove. Forty-five minutes later he was still driving around, north up the Don Valley Highway to the 401 and then south to the Lakeshore, winding his way until he turned onto the Leslie Street Spit. This deserted spit followed a circling path that took the occasional driver and weekend cyclist around its bent frame until the city stood behind them, the CN Tower and Sky Dome dominating the horizon. He stopped his car and got out about three-quarters of the way around the bend. He sat on the car's hood looking back at the city. A large inlet of water came between the spit and the city. Looking through the trees offered one of the most beautiful and little known views of Toronto. Turning around you could see Lake Ontario reaching out into the distance. He had never seen this view before; had never driven on the spit before. It was the wrong day for it. Scott didn't notice anything around him now. All he could see was confusion.

He called home and told Sabrina where he was. She wasn't surprised, and that in itself made Scott realize how far away from himself he must have been over that last while. Sabrina knew that something was going to break soon; she was concerned. "Honey, are you going to be all right?"

"Yes, I am." He sounded much more confident than he felt, which was almost always the case with him. "I'm going back into the office tonight and I hope to get out from under in a few days." Scott knew he had said those words before. Likely the exact same words. He meant them each time, but it never worked out that way. "I love you, Sabrina."

"I love you too, Scott. Please take care of yourself," she said as she hung up.

When Scott got back into the office, everyone had left. He sat down and started working his way through the pile on his desk. He had just organized it when Eric poked his head in. Scott nearly jumped through the roof. "I didn't hear you."

"Oh sorry, Scott. Just here to empty your basket."

"Who are you?" Scott blurted out. "Do you keep leaving those crumpled cryptic notes in my basket?"

Eric smiled and slowly sat down in the chair against the wall. "It doesn't matter, Scott. You asked for a guide and I'm who you have created."

Scott stared at him. Eric returned the stare, a contented smile on his face. They scrutinized each other for a minute or two until Scott finally asked, "Created? What does that mean? I didn't ask for a guide."

"Yes, you did, Scott. You screamed for one. Just not out loud. With every missed soccer game."

"How did you know that?" Scott interrupted. He was getting agitated and spooked. "And it was only one game." he added meekly.

"So far—and that's one hundred percent of Jim's soccer games, Scott." Eric went on, "With every letter of resignation, with every silent walk through your team's room, with every bead of sweat that's dropped from your forehead worrying about getting recognition, with every prepared checklist allocating small tasks you've given people, with every angry, impatient word to Sabrina. With these actions you've begged for a new way to see the world." He paused. "You have reached the point in your life where you first need to change yourself and your view of the world, in order for the world to be changed by you."

Eric paused and looked at Scott a long time, studying his face, then continued. "The route that you took to get here was successful in its own way and for its time in your life, but it will not take you to your next level. It will consistently cause you, and others around you, pain."

Scott was confused. Who was this garbage person who knew the intimate details of his life, pronouncing judgment on them? The scariest part of this discussion was that Eric was right. That hurt—the idea that it was Scott who was causing pain to himself and others. He had images of Jim and Sabrina, Rick, Jessie, John and Emma and of the others he was still working with. Defensively, he answered: "What route are you talking about?"

"Checklists. Boxes. X's and O's. Numbers. Facts and figures, Scott. Just add more to your plate. Just make lists longer and then one by one check them off until you're done. Isn't that what you're doing tonight?"

"Well, those things are part of my job, and..." Scott tried to protest, but Eric kept going.

"That, and walking past people. You're good at that, Scott. You walk right past them as if they were desks or chairs—obstacles that could slow you down in your quest for the perfect and direct line from here to your constantly elusive and ever-changing there. Scott, I don't want to argue with you. That's not my role. Whether you know it or not, you asked me to come here. The way I look at it, if you want to argue for your garbage, you get to keep it. I'll just go to another office, that's all."

Scott moved back. Suddenly the effort to hold it all together caught up with him. He was just too tired—too tired to protest; to make sense of everything, to deny what he was experiencing. His body sagged into the soft contours of the chair, as if he were a weak branch bending under the weight of a vulture. He had no idea who this person was or what was going on but he knew he was right. It hurt to hear the truth, but Scott was simply too tired to protest and throw up all of the rational defenses he had used his whole life.

"You've known for a long time that lists can be made infinitely longer, but your capacity to manage them is finite. You need a new way to see the world of work, Scott, in order for you to be able to manage it. The complexity of your world is getting beyond the tools you have successfully used in the past. And the first step to getting help was asking for a guide. When you asked, I came."

"I don't remember asking. When did I ask?" Scott was resigning himself to the fact that this person, whoever he was, was there, that this conversation was taking place.

"On the dock, Scott. When you were standing on the Leuty dock looking at the boats come out from Ashbridge's Bay, you knew in your heart that you were ready to find a different way to look at the world. You just didn't know how. Your first step was acknowledging that, Scott. It's the biggest step."

"I don't get it. Why there? Why did I contact you there?" Scott was still trying to find a logical sequence in this.

Eric laughed. "Well, it's not like I have all the answers, my friend. Perhaps it was the contrast. It happens that way sometimes."

"What contrast?" Scott asked.

"Remember that night on the dock when the wind on the water was so high? Remember the water? The sailboats racing out of Ashbridge's Bay, their colorful spinnakers dancing with life and vibrancy, their adventurous lungs filled with a strong wind and an urgent need to move? All around you was energy, life and beauty, so much endless beauty, Scott." Eric paused as if he could see it all and was enjoying the view in a way Scott had not —even at the time. "You could see it, Scott, but you couldn't feel it. And somewhere inside you was a distant echo, somewhere inside you could still remember that you had once been able to feel that beauty. That's often the first stage, Scott, when you spot a gap between what you can see and what you can feel. When that happens you are being reminded, through your pain, that you are losing parts of yourself. Big parts, Scott. The next stage—you aren't there yet, but you're slipping in and out of it—is when you can't even see the beauty. You numb yourself to some of the pain at this stage, Scott. But not all of it, and the pain that's left is relentless. That's when it's much harder to find a guide. It's still possible, but much harder," Eric said, lowering and shaking the matted gray hair on the top of his round head, as if he had personally witnessed those who had slipped past this point.

Eric looked up after a moment. "But there's no use in you or me or anyone trying to put more information in, when you've dedicated your life to filling yourself up already. At some point we all realize that some of the stuff that we've always believed about the world will hold us back from experiencing it for what it really is. When your can is full of garbage, Scott, don't throw in more. Dump it out."

He picked up Scott's over-full wastebasket and emptied it into his bag and handed it back. Scott glanced down and there it was, another parchment crunched up in a ball: "But keep some of it," Eric said with a wink.

Scott mustered one last protest from his tired but still fighting brain. "This is crazy. You don't exist. No one here has heard of you. They think I'm crazy for asking about you."

"Well, don't ask Scott. You don't need to confirm your own experience with others. That's another thing, this validating your experience with others. You've done it too much, my tired friend. People will see only what they are ready to see."

"Why am I ready to see you?"

"Because you have had enough of generating your own pain."

"What pain?"

"The pain that comes again and again from banging your head against the same 'soft' issues. The pain is a wake-up call for you to pay attention, Scott. To, not miss the present. To let yourself experience whatever it is you're experiencing. If you're wise your experience will be your teacher, Scott."

"You said that before," Scott replied. "On the parchment. Something like, 'You will learn from wisdom or experience. It is your choice.' What did you mean by that?"

"Experience will teach you and everyone sooner or later Scott. That is just the way it is. Whether you want to learn or not. The problem is that it's painful; experience is really persistent about bringing you back for another lesson, and another, until you get it. Some don't learn until they look back on their life from their deathbed. Some learn sooner, but much later than they need. Others, a few, learn these lessons along the way—when they have had enough of the pain and want to learn a different way."

"Through wisdom?" offered Scott.

"Yes, through wisdom. Wisdom comes from paying attention to experience at the time. Seeing it. Feeling it. Finding the meaning in it. Being fully present for long enough in the here and now to get the lesson." He paused for a long time, then continued. "It doesn't mean you avoid pain. You do the opposite. You look right at the things that cause you pain, you look without wincing and without blinking, you learn from them honestly and without blame or hostility toward others, and then you let them go. Only by having the courage to learn the lesson that experience is here to teach you—today can you stop experience from having to teach you again."

"What are the lessons I need to get now?"

"That soft is hard. That you have reached the level in your development, both personally and professionally, where you can no longer deal with the world through the lens of facts and figures. That lens has served its purpose and still has a place in your world, but alone it clouds more than it discloses. Your lens has to change."

"To what?"

"To the only things that can make a difference in your world now, Scott." Eric got up and started walking down the hallway. Scott followed, knowing that in a moment the janitor would be gone.

"To what?" asked Scott, wanting an answer before Eric left. Even if he didn't know what this thing was all about, he needed to hear what Eric was going to say.

"To what is real." Eric said without turning around.

"What *is* real?" Scott yelled down the wall.

"That's for you to learn, through wisdom or experience. It's your choice." Eric turned around the corner of the cubicles at the end of the hallway and all was silent. No footsteps. No door closing. Just silence and a slight breeze that came and went almost imperceptibly.

Scott walked back into his office and took the crumbled paper out of the basket and smoothed it on the top of his desk. He stared at the words for a long time.

Management Lesson Number Two

You have reached the place in your life where you first have to change yourself and your view of the world, in order for the world to be changed by you.

The stuff that you have always believed about the world is precisely what will hold you back from experiencing it for what it really is.

When your can is full of garbage, dump it out.

chapter seven

The Incredible Disappearing Manager

"The intellect has little to do on the road to discovery. There comes a leap in consciousness, call it intuition or what you will and the solution comes to you and you don't know how or why. All great discoveries are made in this way."
—*Albert Einstein*

"It's Mary Binacotti on the phone for you, Scott. Can you take the call?" Joanne called from her desk.

Scott felt a bit jittery. Why would I be nervous with this client on a phone call? "Yes, put her through."

"Hi, Mary." His voice was overly enthusiastic, he thought.

"Hi, Scott. Just calling to catch up and find out where you guys are at with the process you said you'd put in place. We're looking forward to reviewing it with you and your team." She almost beamed over the phone.

That was it. That was why he was nervous, Scott realized. He knew that he couldn't keep up the level of enthusiasm that

Mary had and it made him nervous. He knew that on some level, no matter how he expressed it, he should be the most enthusiastic promoter of what Replico did. But he wasn't, and it didn't matter how much of a facade he put on. He couldn't match the genuine article.

"We've put together a team," he almost said 'committee' but caught himself, "on this, Mary, and we're looking at ways we can integrate our functions to better meet your needs." Scott managed to sound professional, he thought.

There was a bit of a pause. Just a slight one. "Okay, Scott. Looking forward to hearing what you come up with. When do you think our team can expect a presentation from yours?"

Scott pulled out a piece of paper from under the mess on his desk. He quickly ran his finger down the list and said, "We'll have a process document to you in a week, and the final presentation and pitch will be the third week of August if that works for your team." That was a week before her deadline for presentations. Scott had set an early deadline for himself and the team to show that they didn't need all the time Mary had given them. That was ambitious, he knew. It gave his team around three months to prepare the kind of detail that would be required to form this level of relationship with the kinds of resource commitments it would take. He wondered, even as he said it, whether he would regret it when they were up against the deadline.

"Excellent, Scott. I'll follow up to book your presentation time with our team here in our headquarters. I'm sure it will be exciting. I took a look at some of your company's earlier work on pirate ships. It was impressive."

How did she get her hands on that? Scott wondered suspiciously. It couldn't have been through an Internet search. Either she'd seen the company's old models or early product materials. "Oh, great." he said, trying to sound casual. "How'd you get the material?"

"Jameela sent me some old product information the other day. It was great."

Jameela! What kind of stunt was this? First she sends her assistant to a meeting with me, and now she does an end run right into my client's office. Does she want to run this project? Is that what this is all about? Scott was livid. His face was starting to flush. "That's great. Jameela is a real help," he said quietly into the phone. "If you need anything else, just call me and I'll make sure you get it."

He managed to keep himself together long enough to end the conversation on a relatively high note. He was dialing Jameela's phone number almost before he hung up.

"Hi, Scott it's Katrina. How can I help you?" Her voice reminded him of Mary's, and it bothered him.

"Put me through to your boss." He didn't have the time or patience for small talk right now.

He got Jameela's voice mail, which made him even madder. When he heard the beep, he was like a racehorse let out of the gate. "Jameela. What the hell is going on? I just got off the phone with Binacotti, and she says that you've been in contact with her and sent her product information. How am I supposed to manage the client relationship if you're interfering? I didn't appreciate you sending Katrina to an important meeting, and I don't appreciate this effort to undermine me with the client." He ranted on a bit longer and then slammed the phone down.

He didn't like to have to do that, even though he was boiling mad. But at some point he had to let people know that he wasn't to be ignored and taken advantage of.

Scott sat stewing in his own juices for the next few minutes until he heard a knock on his open door. He suddenly realized that his yelling on the phone could have been clearly heard outside his office. John was at his door.

"Come on in, John." Scott said.

"If you don't have the time now, we can set up a time later," he said. "I just saw that your door was open."

Scott thought that John more honestly could have said that he'd *heard* that his door was open. "No, let's do it now, John. What is it?" Scott said.

"I've signed a contract with the new supplier. They'll be expensive at this late date, but I think they'll work for this project, and for others in the future. What I really want to talk to you about is taking on more responsibility. I'd like to take over some of Jessie's old responsibilities. I think I'm ready."

This would mean a promotion for John. While he and Jessie had been on the same level, they were on different pay scales. Scott stood up, walked over and closed the door. As he sat back down, he said, more patiently than he thought he could, "John, I appreciate that, and your willingness to take that on. It's been a tough year for the team and the evaluations were less than wonderful for almost everyone. But the only one on the team who has performed at a level worthy of promotion is Emma."

John's expression didn't so much change as disappear. His face went blank. Scott continued. This was a good opportunity, Scott thought, to motivate John. "John, I need you to round out your abilities. You show great promise in some areas, but in others you need to improve substantially. This isn't just about you—almost everyone on the team is in the same boat." Scott was trying to be diplomatic, and he congratulated himself for this. Scott had, for the moment, forgotten about Jameela. Right now, all his pent-up anxiety was focused on John and this opportunity to coach and motivate, and for a time, to forget about his own problems. Scott was addicted to crisis—he erased the blasting pain of the last crisis with the siren's song of the new.

The problem with the whole team, Scott was sure, was that each member was lagging in some areas. Scott had tried, tactfully, to influence each of them when he had first taken over the job. He'd tried to get each to see what an opportunity they would have as a team if they improved on their weaknesses. He lined up courses that were ignored, and speakers who were criticized, and he even offered what little incentives he could at his level. Nothing. Nothing, except the realization that they couldn't stand his constant, determined, persistent effort to improve. Only Emma had responded with flying colors on all fronts, and he was not going to let any promotion within his team, no matter how small, go to anyone else. That would spell the death of his control, Scott knew.

"I am ready and qualified for that job, Scott," John protested. "I don't think Emma can do it as well as I can."

The frustration Scott had felt before the call rushed back in. He didn't appreciate the protest. Didn't appreciate that no one, *no one* appreciated his efforts to do what was right—to reward performance, not politics. Don't test me today, John, Scott said to himself, because I will blow you out of this office with both barrels.

John tried to talk, but Scott wouldn't let him. "The best indicator of future success, John, is past performance. That's not something I made up. It is researched. So don't give me the line that Emma doesn't deserve it. She performs, John, better than you, and consistently." Scott rose out of his chair, opening the door for John to leave, which he eventually did after remaining seated for an uncomfortably long time, shaking his head and staring at Scott.

When John left, Scott felt himself cave in. Whatever holds a person up, allows him or her to stand and not fall over, to carry weight, to hold an opinion—whatever it is that defines what he or she is and is not—all of it started to buckle and sway. The room swirled for a moment; Scott felt a mild pain in his chest and sank into his chair, slumped to his right. Is this a heart attack, he wondered. He breathed deeply, believing that he could tell if it was muscular. It hurt more when he expanded his lungs. He was just hurting, not dying, he decided. Too much stress.

As he sat there, with his eyes closed and breathing deeply, Scott perceived an image of himself. It was if he was outside and floating above himself, seeing himself sitting in his chair. But, as he watched, the person in the chair got smaller and smaller. It was as if each pressure, each betrayal, each fight and friction took away a bit of him until there was nothing left; but an empty black chair and an overfull desk.

Nothing seems to be going right. I'm not getting any support. Everyone is playing politics. My team keeps asking for assignments they haven't earned, and they're screwing up their current jobs—but meticulously documenting their legal cases. The company is heading in a direction it may not be able to take. I'm responsible for a cross-functional team that not only doesn't report to me, they ignore and undermine me. Scott felt isolated, confused and afraid. I'm the incredible disappearing manager, thought Scott. What's happening to me?

Scott stood up and looked out the window at the gray parking lot and the grayer still day. The more he thought about it, the more he realized it was true. He hadn't felt merely nervous when he talked to Mary Binacotti; he'd felt exposed. Genuine enthusiasm highlights its opposite in uncomfortable relief.

Scott knew he had to work late again. He couldn't find any way out of the cycle. However, Scott had another reason for wanting to work late: He wanted to see if *he* would show up again.

He didn't have to wait long. Soon after the last employee had gone, Scott could hear a shuffling in the hallway. Eric walked right in and took Scott's basket, not saying a word.

"No hello tonight, Eric?"

"Hello, Scott. Just thought since I don't exist I would just empty your basket and split without threatening your logic."

This made Scott laugh. He caught himself and started questioning Eric again, "Who are you, and how do you get in here?"

"Scott, I think we've covered this before. If you don't want me to show up, then why did you wait for me this evening? You don't have to answer that, Scott. I'll go. As I said, Scott, you can keep your garbage, if you argue for it." Eric put the full garbage can on the floor and turned to go."

"No!" Scott yelled. Eric turned and Scott controlled himself. "No, don't go," he said more quietly. "I don't care who you are, I need help," he said with resignation.

Eric turned and emptied the basket then handed it back. Eric sat down and Scott noticed the paper ball. Scott put the basket back near his desk and decided to open the paper later when Eric was gone, respecting the small tradition that had grown between them.

"I need help." Scott repeated, this time so that he could listen to the words.

"Yes, you do, Scott. Lots of it. But not from me, my friend."

"What do you mean? Isn't that why you're here?" Scott was confused.

Eric didn't reply. "Isn't it getting tiring, fighting that war, Scott?"

"What war? What are you talking about?"

"You against the world. You can't trust anyone, can't rely on anyone, can't let yourself be off guard with anyone, can't share your doubts with anyone, can't be real with anyone, can't make a mistake in front of anyone. Isn't it getting tiring, being the only one you can count on?"

"Well, lately I can't count on myself either. I don't know what's happening to me. I don't recognize myself. I'm disappearing."

Neither spoke for a while. Eric was looking at Scott as if measuring him for what he was going to say, and then deciding, almost reluctantly, to speak. "Scott, if you disappear, you are the last one to go. Others have disappeared for you long ago." He paused for a moment. "It may get harder before it gets easier."

"I can't imagine it getting harder, Eric. I can't go on like this."

"You have to do one thing that's going to make you seem like you're getting farther behind. Something that you should have done long ago, and all along."

"What's that?"

"Take the time to get to know yourself. And get to know the people in your life, some for the first time. Stop. Look. Listen to yourself and others, Scott."

"How? When can I make the time? What will I do? How will it help? Who do I start with?" Scott was already trying to make a mental checklist, and this gave him a brief shot of energy. Then another thought took that energy away. He realized how unlikely it was that the people in his life would be open to his advances to get to know them.

Eric commented as if he could read Scott's mind. "Scott, you have to stop giving up your power and disappearing. No one can make you disappear except yourself. You can't control what others will do, but you can always choose how you will react." He looked at Scott as if he were looking into his soul. "No one can take that from you, Scott."

"The world gets so complicated, so many different pressures pulling me so many ways. How can I know what is the right way to react?"

"That's not until our next lesson, Scott. I'd better go." Eric got up and walked out. He moved slower somehow, standing up cautiously as if his back was bothering him. Eric continued, "For now, work on this one."

Management Lesson Number Three

Stop, look and listen —
to yourself and others.

You can't control what others will do.
Your power is won or lost in
how you **choose** to react.

chapter eight

Meaning

"The trouble with music appreciation in general is that people are taught to have too much respect for music; they should be taught to love it instead."
—*Igor Stranvinsky*

Scott woke early Monday morning and dressed, while Sabrina still slept. He kissed her gently on the cheek and pulled the sheets closer to her, tucking them under her chin and rubbing her back. She didn't open her eyes, but managed a mumbled "Love you."

"I love you too, sweetie." He walked down the three floors, stopping on the second to kiss Jim goodbye.

Scott dressed warmly and took a cup of very hot coffee with him as he left. He headed for the beach and toward the Leuty Lifeguard Station. He wanted to try to take a few moments to connect with himself again, to try to stop, look and listen, even if just for a few moments before work, to see what might come up. It was the third week of May and he already felt the deadline three months off but he was determined to choose a different path to approach this challenge.

Only a few runners were out this early. They nodded as they passed, barely moving their heads. The lights were still on in the old-fashioned lampposts that Sabrina liked so much. Their pale blue color reminded Scott of the basketball team, the St. Agnes Steelers, that he played on in his high school years growing up in Halifax. The east coast city—in fact, the whole province of Nova Scotia—was crazy for basketball. Across Canada, hockey reined supreme, but in Halifax ten thousand knowledgeable fans would pour into the Metro Centre to see a university basketball game. This was unheard of in the rest of the country. Scott had been a fanatic.

The baby-blue and maroon uniforms of the Steelers had been a highlight of his youth. The memories of this church-league team flooded back to him as he walked east along the boardwalk. There had been tremendous lessons in those years for him. It wasn't something that he talked about a lot, but it had impressed him greatly. Somehow the coach, Nick Morash, had breathed life into a small church gym and a bunch of kids. He had taken very ordinary conditions and created, through passion, effort and sheer love of the game, an environment that, over time, had tremendous meaning for Scott and the others.

Everybody had a role on the Steelers, Scott remembered. Not everyone got to do everything he wanted but everyone got to contribute. The bench player, who was expected to make the key pick, was a hero and so was the scorer who helped win the game. The way you practiced, worked and played mattered. Everyone's efforts were connected and the team won or lost together.

There was a pride that developed with being a Steeler. The small church gym was transformed into a place of practice, effort, focus, commitment and teamwork, and on occasion, a packed showcase for great games. The Steelers started to attract talented kids from around the city, from the Canadian Martyrs Church, and from the west and east of the city. The lessons were many, Scott remembered, but the one that came back clearly was this: Nick had taken something that had started out without any real sense of mission, basketball at St. Agnes Church, and turned it into something that many would work extremely hard for, something that had meaning beyond the game itself. How, Scott wondered. Why can't I do this for my own team? Why haven't I thought about this for so long? Why now?

It was still dark when Scott reached the lifeguard station, pulled himself up on the raised dock and walked down to the end. It was surrounded on two sides by the rocks and sand that stretched out to the lake. Behind him was the white-washed wall of the station, with its red perch on top where the lifeguards sat and surveyed the water.

Mornings used to be his favorite part of the day. Getting out before others made the day seem to stretch on infinitely, pregnant with possibility and hope. It was the same feeling he had had in grade school just before summer vacation. Time was endless. His attention was acute. Every minute mattered, and he had noticed; everything. As he walked up the dock he thought about how, as a child, he could never simply walk from home to school or to the store and back. Everything had had nuance. Curbs weren't simply to be walked over or on; he had noticed their thickness and texture. He had explored each new experience. Perhaps it's that quality, he thought, as he sat against the chipped, warped boards, the attention to the here and now—that creates more time, that turns the finite into the infinite. Maybe focused attention creates the peace that comes with feeling infinite possibility, that clears the mind of the well-worn ruts of the expert's perceived perfection. Venture turned into an adventure through attention and curiosity.

The air always felt cleaner in the early mornings, and the chill gave it a crispness that he could feel roll down his throat and deep into his lungs. So much of what you bring into yourself you choose, he thought, as he drank in the dawn, something he hadn't tasted since moving to the Beach. He realized that he had lost the pleasure of the morning long ago—along with so many other pleasures.

But for now, the experience of the moment, that moment, flowed through him, like blood carrying oxygen to every life-breathing cell of his soul. The dawning morning of infinite grace, the speckled sand and cool, sure water, the well-worn boards of the dock that lined up like railway tracks leading to the water's edge—the present moment, the beauty he saw all around him was the same as the beauty he felt inside.

A while later, Scott climbed down from the dock and walked east, the sun reflecting off him onto the boardwalk, dancing with him as he, without hurry, made his way into work.

"Joanne, can I have a word with you in my office when you're free?" Scott asked when she walked in later than usual. Scott knew that normally he would have reacted negatively to her lateness, and a part of him still wanted to.

When she sat down, Scott could see she was anticipating his usual reaction to her late arrival. "I've noticed you've been late a lot recently, Joanne," he began. She visibly tensed, "I was just wondering if everything is okay," Scott continued. "Is there anything that I might be able to do?" Scott could hear himself talking, but it didn't sound like him. He felt almost phony and struggled to keep his sarcastic tone in check.

Joanne's rigid back relaxed. She took her time answering, as if considering a fork in a road. "Thank you," she replied, finally. "I'll try to get in on time Scott. I've just been having a few problems with Heather. She's been sick lately and missing a lot of school."

"I'm sorry to hear that, is there anything that I can do?"

She hesitated and look at him for a moment, then replied, "No, thank you though, it will work out."

"I also wanted to talk to you about your request to get involved in the project proposal. I'd like you to take it on." He was twisting his pencil nervously as he spoke. "But with Heather please don't feel that you need to take this on right now. I just want you to know that I think you would do a good job of it."

Joanne leaned forward as if straining to pick up a part of the message that she'd missed. When she was sure she had heard correctly she walked out of his office. She returned and put a plan on his desk without saying a word. Joanne was enjoying the moment fully. "I can start to implement it as soon as I get some feedback on it." Joanne looked down at him and said, "Thank you."

She was very controlled, but sincere. Appropriate, thought Scott.

As Joanne left, he asked her to call Emma into a meeting. He had delayed dealing with the vacancy left by Jessie for too long. No new hire was going to fill that void, and they paid the price for that lost expertise daily.

By the end of the day, Scott had given Emma most of Jessie's old responsibilities. It was a slight promotion and the added pay, while small, would help Emma. She had been quite clear that the pay raise was what she wanted. She was grateful but more nervous than Scott had expected, given her stellar track record and experience.

Scott made more decisions that morning than he had made in the previous five days. When the day was over, he felt that he was finally moving his agenda forward. But each new responsibility that he passed on to others generated its own new obligations for him. His own to-do list got longer and longer, so that by Wednesday, the Monday morning on the dock seemed like a distant memory. Once again, he was running out the door trying to save time. By Thursday, he was buried again behind mounds of paper. The more he tried to let go, to stop, look and listen—the less he actually got done. The pressures didn't decrease; they grew.

He pulled into the garage Thursday evening around seven thirty. The lights in the kitchen were on, and as he came through the back door, he could see Jim sitting on the chair getting ready to be read a story. Scott was so tired he was scuffing the toes of his shoes as he walked. "Daddy, can you read me a story?" Jim called out.

"Sure son. Just let me get my coat off." Jim kissed Sabrina, and she could feel the tension in his body. "Sorry to be late, sweetie. It's John again." They chatted for a little while before Scott settled into one of the two big chairs and pulled Jim onto his lap. Jim was holding a book on pirates.

"Dad, I saw the pirates again at the beach today." He beamed and passed the book to Scott.

Scott gave Sabrina a quick glance. She stared back "Jim, son, this is a great pretend book, but there are no pirates down at our beach." He said it as gently as he could. "They're not real, Jim. You just make them up in your imagination." As Sabrina stormed out of the room, he added, "but imagination's a good thing Jim."

Scott started reading. Jim asked for only one page and then slipped off his dad's lap and went upstairs with Sabrina. Scrunched in a ball into a corner of the chair, Scott fell into an uncomfortable sleep before Jim reached the second floor.

Friday was even worse. The work that Joanne was giving him was bad. John appeared to resent Emma's new responsibilities, and even Emma was not herself. The silence was thunderous sometimes, and by the end of the day, Scott badly wanted to leave the building. But he couldn't. He would work late into the evening.

He was about to leave when Eric walked into his office. Scott immediately reached for his wastebasket and handed it to him. Neither spoke. Scott didn't know what to say. He was trying to accomplish some things that seemed, on the surface, good—but nothing was getting better.

Eric could sense it. Before either of them could even say hello, Eric handed Scott the basket, a crumbled ball now in it. "It gets harder before it gets easier, Scott. I told you that."

"But the more I delegate from my lists, it seems my lists just get longer. I not only have to redo the work, I have to transfer it, explain it, re-answer and explain it again. I've tried to listen to myself and others, but it's eating up my time and, as usual, the only time I can get through my own lists is at night. So here I am again; I don't want to work late but here I am."

Eric nodded and sat down. "I understand. I've been there."

That was the first time that Eric had revealed anything about himself.

"Do you have any questions for me?" Eric continued.

Scott had wanted to run into Eric tonight, even though there was no specific problem he wanted to focus on. For a long time he sat there and looked at his desk, flipping through page after page of notes and lists. Eric just sat and looked on with interest, as if he were watching Homo Corporatus—part human, part machine, that not-at-all rare, but curiously strange creature that cages himself.

It was in the middle of the to-do list, exactly in the middle of the hundreds of future commitments, that Scott realized what he needed to know. If he was to make a difference as a manager in the constant ebb and flow of events, if he was to affect others in a positive way, he had to understand how to make some decisions—positive decisions that he could live with, he had to learn to make these decisions even when he didn't have enough information or time, and when the circumstances were complex or bore no resemblance to the ones that he had signed on for. "How can I make sense out of chaos and still move myself, my team and my company forward?" That's what he wanted to ask the janitor.

When Eric heard Scott's question, a smile crossed his face as if he had waited for this for some time. His voice was confident and he answered immediately. It was clear from the first word that Eric had somehow lived this question. Scott wondered whether he had ever been a manager.

"When you are surrounded by chaos, ask yourself one question and one question only: Are the choices you are making leading yourself and others toward meaning?" Eric looked at Scott for a long time, and then went on, "If they are, continue; if they are not, stop."

Scott didn't react quickly, but when he did, he showed his disappointment. "Listen, Eric, I'm not sure if you've managed others, but it's not my job to provide meaning to my staff. I just need to get the job done. That's it. That's what I'm paid for, and ..."

But Eric finished the sentence for him, "and you are finding that your current ways of thinking about work, don't work."

"Well, that wasn't what I was going to say exactly, but that is true. The way I work isn't working." Scott had waited for the words; but when he finally heard them, he didn't see their practical application. "Eric, I just have workers, half of whom are union and half not. They don't want to walk into my office and have their manager, *me*," he was picturing himself standing in front of his team and cringing, "ask them, 'Did you find *meaning* in your work today?' I'd be laughed out of the office."

Eric laughed, then he spoke in a voice that Scott hadn't heard before, a voice that was both sure and confident yet filled with tenderness and dusted lightly with regret, perhaps even sadness. "Every one of them, without exception, yearns to feel that their work has meaning, Scott. That the way they make their choices, direct their tasks, infuse their energy, spend their minutes, hours, days—their lives—makes a difference to others: to their colleagues, their employer, their customers, their families." It was as if it wasn't a voice at all; it was an echo. A distant and fading reflection of countless voices from countless moments in countless lives.

"It's your inability to understand how profound that need is in each and every one, that stops you from allowing your team to make choices that would increase meaning for them and increase productivity and performance for all."

Scott waited for a moment. Then he reacted with defensiveness. Something about this, more than anything Eric had said or given him to date, struck a nerve. "I am not a counselor. I'm a manager. I have to get a job done. We do proposals. We win jobs. We satisfy customer needs while managing people who have a million agendas that don't always work for the company's interest. This isn't an ideal world, Eric!"

"Fine, Scott. I told you my role is not to argue with you. You can keep your garbage. Remember, Scott, what one of the first lessons said."

Scott pulled out the papers from his drawer. "Pay attention!" he read aloud.

"That's it, Scott. Pay attention—to your experience. You will see that keeping your distrustful nature will result in building distrust. Choosing a different reaction to the world will lead to different outcomes. You can have another outcome. It's your choice." He paused and grinned, "In this restaurant I would recommend that you try a new dish; your regular never was very satisfying."

"No, it wasn't and isn't, Eric." Scott hesitated as if he wanted to say something and then stopped. Then he started again and his mouth opened. But once more, he stopped.

Eric looked at him. "It's okay, Scott. I know what you're going to say. You don't have to say it."

"Yes, I do. You're right about what others need; I know that I've lost out as well. I need to find meaning again in my work. I need to believe I'm making a difference, that all the time I put into my work will add up to something worthwhile for myself and others here," he looked away from Eric and up at a pirate ship in a bottle sitting on top of his file cabinet and then at the picture of Sabrina and Jim sitting on the corner of his desk, "and at home. I don't know where I started to lose that feeling, but I know it's gone."

Eric stretched his legs. "You'll not be able to create environments in which others can find meaning for themselves, unless you find it for yourself along the way."

Scott's voice had changed. It was as if it wasn't a voice at all, but a tender, slightly dusty echo. "I know."

Management Lesson Number Four

When you are surrounded by chaos, ask
yourself one question and one question only:

Are the choices you are making leading
yourself and others toward meaning?
If they are, continue; if they are not, stop.

People need to feel they are moving from
relative levels of chaos and isolation toward
higher levels of order and community. In the
combinations and permutations of those
movements they find meaning.

part three

Walk Softly and Carry a Big Idea!

"There is a loftier ambition than merely to

stand high in the world. It is to stoop down

and lift mankind a little higher."

—*Henry Van Dyke*

chapter nine

Jump!

"Life is either a daring adventure, or it is nothing."
—Helen Keller

Scott had walked to work again and he could feel the early morning air start to get warmer as June approached. He was consistently taking the few extra minutes for himself now. Today he had chosen to walk down Queen Street rather than the boardwalk. The eclectic mix of two-story shops, bookstores and restaurants and converted older homes, combined with the long beach and boardwalk, made the Beach community a favorite destination for Torontonians on hot summer days. On weekends Queen Street East was packed from Scott's house at Woodbine all the way to Replico, and it was a challenge for the most eastern of the local residents to escape the Beach by car. At this time in the morning, on his way to work, there was only a smattering of cars easily working their way west and out of the Beach. He was happy to be on foot.

Scott stopped in a local coffee shop, picked up a coffee for himself and walked out. Then he quickly turned and went back in. He bought a second cup, putting an extra sugar and milk in his pocket, though he wasn't sure they were needed. Ten minutes later he dropped it off on Joanne's desk, but thought it would be too cold when she came in. He was right.

Joanne came in just before nine, and seemed very disturbed. When she noticed the cup, he explained that he had been in much earlier and thought she might like it. Scott could see the worry in her face and asked her to step in his office.

He was glad that he had asked Joanne about her lateness. Scott at least understood that there were some things affecting Joanne. He didn't like this part of his job, the part that involved what he would have to tell Joanne today. She had done the resource plan for RRI and it was adequate at best. He would have to put a lot of time into it, almost as much as if he had done it himself. But inside Joanne's plan, Scott noticed something that surprised him. She had done an exceptional job of the financial review. Although that section was not a big one in the resource plan at this stage, the detail and structure was, for her level of experience, surprisingly good. Scott knew that she wanted to be responsible for the whole plan, but in his best judgment, that was not in anyone's best interest at this time.

Joanne sat down and Scott closed the door. "What is it Joanne? Is your little one okay?" It really bothered him that he couldn't remember her daughter's name. He should know it, but it just wouldn't come to mind.

"Heather is going to have to go to the hospital. The doctors say she's likely fine, but they'll admit her in a few days for some testing." Joanne started crying.

Scott didn't know what to do or say. A part of him wanted to go over, put an arm around her and comfort her; he kicked himself for glancing at the closed door. He sat there. "I'm so sorry, Joanne. Is there anything I, or anyone here can do? Would you like to take today off?" Even as he was saying it, he was thinking about the day ahead and how they would cover for her. Scott quickly realized that they wouldn't be able to. Not today. Still he sat there.

"No, that's okay, Scott. Thank you. I'll be fine. I just needed to tell someone. Frank is at home with Heather, but I'll need to take some time off next week. That could interfere with the RRI Resource Plan a bit—I've been thinking about that a lot and how to cover for it."

There was no way he was going to wade into that discussion now, later, if she was up for it. "We can talk about all that later, Joanne. Don't worry about it now." He wanted to change his evaluation of the RRI Project Plan, but he didn't. Couldn't. He just didn't want to have to tell her.

That afternoon Joanne put the RRI folder on his desk, saying "When you want to, Scott, let's talk about this."

He was relieved that she initiated the discussion. He really had to move the project forward soon. "Right now is fine." He put his pen down and brought out his own agenda with notes on the project.

He didn't know how to start, so he asked her a question. "How was it for you putting this together?"

Joanne sat up in her chair. She seemed energetic and focused. "I enjoyed most of it, and I think I've done a good job. I found some of it difficult, especially initially trying to get the input from so many people. What did you think of it?"

There was the question. "I really appreciated your initiative, Joanne. We can use the plan with some edits from me and maybe from Ching. I saw something really positive in there; what part of working on the plan felt most natural to you?"

"The financials. I loved it."

Like a carnival magician, Scott held up his agenda paper. On it he'd spelled out in large block letters, "Financial Clarity."

"Do you know how hard it is for most people to make the complexity of the numbers in here as understandable and usable as you did?" he asked brandishing the agenda in the air.

Joanne raised her eyebrows. "No. I just did it and enjoyed it."

"Joanne, most people couldn't do that," Scott told her. "I think that making sense of numbers is one of your true talents. I would like to look at how we could develop that talent and use it more in our team."

Joanne looked clearly pleased and a bit shocked. "What about the whole plan though, Scott? How do you want to proceed?"

"I'd like to finish the plan myself. It needs a bit more structure and I think at this stage, this isn't the right project for you to manage. It just isn't the right fit, Joanne."

Joanne looked very disappointed, although really her expression didn't change but fixed unnaturally in place as she looked away and out the window. This didn't surprise Scott. He was disappointed as well.

"I see. Okay. Well, thanks for letting me try it." She got up out of her chair and walked toward the door.

How could so many emotions surge through this room in such a short time, Scott wondered? He could provide more detailed feedback, if she wanted it, but that wouldn't be now. Sometimes he didn't like being a manager at all.

The days stretched into weeks, and the weeks into a month filled with highs and lows. As July approached he realized that the August presentation would only be just around the corner. Every day Scott was feeling new emotions as he began trying to move himself and his team along. Most surprising to him was Emma. His superstar was not making the transition into her new responsibilities well, and for the first time he was getting negative feedback about her work relationships. That was not the Emma he knew. He had set up a meeting to talk to her about how he could support her transition. He knew Emma had the skills to do the job, so he didn't know what the problem was.

They met in his office for over two hours. He had scheduled one hour, but it was apparent that they needed the time to talk. Emma was better able than most on the team to tell him when he was off track and to get away with it, and she took that opportunity today. He thought it was going to be a meeting about her. It started there but quickly became a chance for Emma to give Scott some feedback.

"People see that you're trying to get them more involved, and they are taking you up on that. But when they start stuff and make the decisions, they don't feel like they have any way of knowing if they're going in the right direction for the medium to long term. We feel like we're operating on a four-month projection plan rather than with a strategic vision."

That hurt, not because it was way off, but because it was right. There were no thanks for the efforts he'd made to get them more involved. He needed to hear the truth. The atmosphere had not really improved, while the demands on his time had increased exponentially. Unusual for her, Emma was ranting. But she was also being frank, and Scott was hearing things he had felt for awhile. They talked about this and what the team was expecting, and then the discussion came back to her.

"Emma, I've have been surprised by some negative comments from clients who say you've had a few tussles with them. That's not usual for you. Is there anything behind this?"

Scott was surprised when Emma responded in an uncharacteristically defensive manner. Eventually she started to let him in on what was happening. She hated her new role. She never really thought she would like it, but knowing that she'd earned it and could do it, she had felt trapped into taking it on. The new responsibilities required her to work closely with customers, and, while she liked this on occasion, it was not something she wanted to do every day. In the end she had taken the new position to advance financially and perhaps, though he wasn't sure about this, to increase her prestige with the company and the team.

Scott remembered his reaction to John—his outrage that John had thought he could get Jessie's old job without paying his dues. It haunted him as he listened to Emma. When she left he called Human Resources, and went down to their office. They didn't want to see him, but he didn't care. He wasn't going to leave until they listened to what he wanted; he knew that what he was about to request wouldn't be within their normal rules.

Everyday Scott consciously made a point of looking at the connections that were happening among his team. He had set John up with Katrina. After two meetings, Jameela stepped in to meet with John, which surprised Scott. It made his ego-filled protests over meeting with Katrina seem extremely foolish. He was delighted at how excited John was getting to work with Jameela and her team. Scott was energized. Scott would try to take some time each day to pull away from his to-do lists, to look at the broader picture to gain some perspective. Sometimes Scott could see a new level of order emerging from the chaos; sometimes he just saw a lot of confusion. He always thought of Eric at these times, and it surprised Scott that he missed him.

Scott had worked very hard at paying attention, trying to move himself and his team forward on the continuum from isolation to connection and community, and to allow the surface chaos of individual efforts and ideas to form its own natural and strong order underneath. Sometimes, though, it was very hard to make decisions in line with that thinking. As the situations became more complex, with longer and longer lists of competing priorities, the harder it became to make fundamental decisions. He was tempted to give up trying and just dive into the details again. It was as if Scott was addicted to action, the powerful appeal of checking things off. But he didn't fold, and for the last month he had consistently made decisions that were in line with a higher level of order and community.

The result was Scott now had more stress, not less. He was working longer hours. He was over-budget in almost every area. Scott doubted his ability to make good decisions. He questioned whether he even wanted to be connected to Replico any more. Perhaps this was the end of his rope. Scott was just about ready to give up, when his friend walked in and reached for his wastebasket.

Eric looked older. Bending over to pick up the basket, he seemed strained and tired. But when he sat down and said hello, he was the same as ever.

"Thanks for coming. I guess you could feel that I needed some help." Scott said. Scott no longer needed to explain Eric to others or to himself. He was just part of Scott's experience, and Scott wanted to pay attention.

Eric nodded and smiled slightly, pushing the basket back before settling into the chair.

"I've lost it—any connection I might have had to this company, to my team, to most things. I really have tried," Scott stopped himself and looked at Eric, "you likely know this already, but I really have tried to implement some of the messages you've left." Scott glanced down at the basket and noticed the paper ball and the sense of relief just seeing it brought him. "Sometimes it feels like I must be on the right track, I see some improvements in the team. But more often than not, I realize I'm falling behind and that I'm not even managing my own tasks well, let alone managing others."

"I know you're trying, Scott. I admire that. It takes great courage, especially at this stage. You have to jump into the dark. You don't have the confidence for having done it before. I wish I could help you and tell you that I can gently lead you back from the edge. I wish I could tell you that it will be all right simply to stand on the ground you are familiar with, but I can't." Eric paused as if remembering.

"At some point we all stand on that cliff, Scott, our toes curled over the black edge of darkness. We know that we must either jump or be less than we are capable of being." Eric had tears in his eyes. He was remembering something; Scott was sure of it.

"What is my cliff? What do I have to jump into?" Scott asked.

"Your experience has already told you that, Scott." As Eric got up, his right knee cracked loudly, and he walked out the door. All was silent and still, save for a short breeze.

Scott pulled the paper from the basket. Below the usual title, there was one word: "Jump!"
Into what?

Management Lesson Number Five

Jump!

chapter ten

Rock Statues

"What I've dared I've willed ... and what I've willed I'll do."
—Herman Melville

Scott had organized a surprise picnic for Sabrina on the weekend. He had picked up some food and packed a basket and arranged for her mother to stay with Jim. It was a surprise that he put together at the last moment to thank her. He had passed his first anniversary, June 4th, at Replico three weeks ago. He wanted to let Sabrina know that he realized what she had sacrificed over the last year while he worked through the challenges in front of him. He loved Sabrina and never wanted to take that for granted, and he knew that for a time he had done just that.

She was surprised when her mother showed up and then Scott brought out the picnic basket. "Scott, we can take Jim with us." She automatically included Jim in everything.

"That will be great another time, Sabrina, but today this is for just you and I." Jim loved staying with his nana, and was eager for his parents to go so she could start spoiling him.

When Scott and Sabrina reached the beach, they strolled around the point that led to Ashbridge's Bay Sailing Club. They walked together, hand in hand, shoulders rubbing, along the gentle curve of the boardwalk. They were heading just around the middle of the curve, when they came across a number of stacks of rocks. Each collection of rocks was stacked one on top of another, about twenty or twenty-five stacks, each about three or four feet high made up of between six and ten rocks each. They were not simply piled up, but precariously balanced on top of each other at very strange and seemingly impossible angles. Each quite magnificently balancing another rock, equally strangely placed, on top of it.

As they passed, there were about ten university students with someone who looked like their professor walking amongst the stacks. The whole class must have done this as a project, Scott and Sabrina agreed as they walked by. The clear sky set off the deep-blue lake sparkling below.

It was incredible how quickly Scott and Sabrina seemed to go back to feeling as if they were dating, when they had a chance to spend some time alone together. They sat down beside the docks where some boats were moored and spread out a blanket and opened their basket. After arranging the food, Scott brought out a small box and gave it to Sabrina. Inside was a note and a wavy wide band of silver that the artist had discovered to be a bracelet. Scott gave it to Sabrina, a reminder for them both to take some time just for each other.

They spent the afternoon sitting, talking and lying back on the blanket just looking at the sky and saying nothing. Their hands touched more in those few hours than they had in the previous year it seemed. Scott and Sabrina talked about everything: Jim and how he was growing up so fast, their parents, neighbors, when they were going to take a vacation, Sabrina's love of staying at home with Jim and her need to find some space for her own activities, and Replico. Mostly, though, the picnic wasn't about talking as much as it was about realizing that they needed to do this more often, that there was no one in the world with whom they would prefer to spend time with. After a while they packed up, and were ready to leave. Scott pulled Sabrina close to him and they kissed. He held her for a long time and whispered in her ear, as much for himself as for her, "I will never ignore our relationship again, Sabrina, in the way I have over this past year. I love you very much."

"Scott it's okay. You had to work hard this year. I understand."

But Scott knew that it wasn't okay and he held her for a long time and vowed, this time to himself that work would not come before her and Jim. Even as he said it he was worried because he didn't know how to ensure that he could keep his promise. He knew if he couldn't find a way, he would leave Replico. He ran his hand through Sabrina's hair and placed his cheek against hers. "I love you."

As they walked back they passed the stacks of rocks. This time there was only one person; he was moving amongst them, shuffling a few rocks. Scott asked the man, who looked about his own age, if he knew who had made these rock sculptures. "I made them." the man said as he kept on moving rocks.

"But how could you?" Scott asked in amazement.

"Well, I had some help. My wife helped earlier and we've been here about six hours."

Scott and Sabrina were surprised by this. The man and his wife must have been hidden behind the university group as they had surveyed his work. Each pile was an incredible piece of art. Scott showed Sabrina his favorites; they involved the smallest rocks holding together impossibly. In a matter of hours the rocks would be pushed over by kids or dogs.

"Why do you make these?" Scott asked.

"Just enjoy it." The man said. "I love the look of them—and the looks on the people's faces when they find them."

The man told Scott and Sabrina to look at the piles from different angles to appreciate the balance inherent in each rock. Sabrina and Scott started walking through the small maze of sculptures, bending over and twisting, getting closer and pulling back to see them differently each time. They were having fun and were impressed with the simple yet powerful, transient beauty this man and his wife had created.

Scott thought the man must be an artist and asked him what he did for a living.

He replied, "I'm a snowplow driver. Do you want to give it a try?"

Sabrina dove right in. She seemed, after a bit of time, to take to it naturally and was enjoying building her own bit of beauty. Scott started tentatively, picking up medium-sized rocks and trying to balance them. At first nothing worked. After some time, one fell into place quite quickly, then a second and a third, and that was as far as he got. But he felt it—the moment when a rock, at a really weird angle, would say, 'this is it for me.' It fits and knows it, and tells you so; if your hand is sensitive enough to listen and you are patient enough to be able to hear. Scott and Sabrina loved it. And though they only spent about fifteen minutes at it, it was wonderful. Magical. Temporary and timeless. Totally useless and absolutely worthwhile.

Just as they both were standing up and Scott began rubbing the sand off Sabrina, giving her a few extra pats on the bum, Scott suddenly yelled. "That's it!" He jumped up in the air. "That's what I'm after. That's the direction that I have to jump." He almost yelled and got up, "For the love of it!"

Sabrina could tell it was something about work but didn't know what and didn't ask. She just loved to hear enthusiasm in his voice again. She brushed the sand off Scott and pinched his bottom. They began walking back home, Scott's armed draped around her shoulders, feeling like best friends who have just played in the sand together.

When Human Resources finally conceded, it was by now the second week of July and it had not been easy, they sent Scott a note and the three thousand scenarios where his idea would not be permitted, but in this specific case, they would allow him to do it. Scott wasn't sure he would get his way that day when he had gone to their office, immediately after Emma had left his. He had told them he was going to lose one of his best employees if they didn't make an exception for this, but they didn't listen. It was not standard and wouldn't fly. They were very sorry.

He had stood up, taken a few steps toward the door and was about to leave, when he realized that he didn't know what he would return to his office to do. This is my job, he thought, and I'm going to do it whether the company likes it or not. He walked back to the chair he had just left, took off his jacket and sat down. "Yes, I understand your position. Here's mine." He didn't mean to get so passionate, but it just poured out. "We are going to find a way to make this happen together, or I'm going to go to your boss and make it happen without you. And if your boss doesn't like this idea, then I am going to go directly to Bob and I will get it done. This is not about me; it is about someone I represent and I am not going to let this woman down. Not now. And neither is Replico."

The Human Resources woman stared at Scott. She was not impressed. He didn't fit into the system that she and others had worked very hard to create.

"I'm not going away until this starts to move forward." Scott added.

After a brief silence she said, "I will bring this up at our meeting tomorrow morning."

Scott was not satisfied with her response but decided to leave it at that for now. "Thank you. I will talk to you tomorrow." Which he did. He called her before noon the next day and found out that her colleagues agreed with her and that it wouldn't be possible. Scott was furious, but this time he didn't let it show. "What time can I see your boss."

It took him five meetings, six memos and a cancelled appointment with Bob, but he got his way, finally. He had not felt this alive or sure of himself in years, and he was not going to let this go by easily. When he got the letter from Human Resources he called Sabrina. "I got it, for Emma, I got approval." Sabrina loved it when he got excited by his work and shared it with her. It had been so rare over the last year.

"Joanne," he called out. "Can you come in here for a moment?" She came in and sat down. "Joanne, I'm going to be putting the final pitch team together to win the RRI project. You already have the responsibility to put the information together for the look of the presentation, but I'd like you to play a more active role. I want you to head up the financial section of the proposal, not just manage the look of this area, but work with each area of the company to ensure that the type of information is right for the client's needs and not just ours. Your role will be making sense of it from the client's perspective, not just Replico's. It will mean putting in some extra time." Scott knew that Heather was fine and the doctors had said the tests didn't turn up anything. "Can you do that? It will mean that you might have to come with us to be in on the pitch itself."

Joanne had never been part of a pitch team sent in to win business. She'd prepared the materials, but she'd never had primary responsibility on any of the pieces. Scott could see her tentativeness and he continued. "I need you on this. You can pull together and make sense of the various budgets better than I can and frankly, in a clearer way than anyone else on the team. If you do this, we'll be stronger."

Joanne paused and then answered. "Yes. When do we have to get it all together?" Scott could see that she was both nervous and excited, "Thank you." she said.

"Well, when you get the mess that some of the people, including me, will send to you, then you might not be thanking me." They both laughed, but Scott realized that Joanne would have to work extremely hard to do this well on top of her other responsibilities.

"Great. I'll get everyone to funnel their info through you." Let me see your first draft when you've completed it. Here are the requirements from the client." He handed her a stack of papers about four inches thick. She nodded and took it with her. "Please call Emma and ask her to come into my office as soon as possible. Now would be great."

When Emma walked in, Scott was bursting with enthusiasm. "Hi, Emma."

"Hi, Scott." Even her tone had changed since she had taken on Jessie's old position. "Emma, I have some news for you. Human Resources has agreed to let you, only if you want it, take on your old role with the pay scale that goes with the one you now have, but with one condition: You have to serve as an official mentor to designated others." Scott knew that this formalized the role that she loved to play anyway. People would often seek her out for her ideas and expertise.

"You mean I get to do my old job and don't have to..." her voice trailed off. Scott realized as he listened to her how hard this new position and the negative feedback she was getting had been on her. He didn't want it to seem like a demotion so he offered, "Yes, but you will have a new title that will reflect the teams ability to go to you for help, advice and council and that will be part of your structured responsibilities. You will be evaluated on this in your performance review."

"Who will assume the responsibilities I give up?" Before Scott could answer, she offered, "I think John can do that role very well, even though he doesn't have the same experience as I do."

"I agree, Emma. But I would like you to work with him on some of the specifics in that role. I want you to serve as a mentor to him. In some areas, I think he won't need a lot of advice. In others, I can see that he might. I hope that he takes up a lot of your time. The mentor role will not be without its headaches."

Emma started crying. Later she said it was the best thing that had ever happened in her career. She loved her old job and had never wanted a promotion, but she did want increased pay at a level that she felt she deserved and some recognition for the outstanding performance and extra contribution that she regularly made. The only promotion available had been Jessie's and so she took it, although neither her heart nor her talent belonged there.

"That's something I've been doing informally for years, and believe me, I know that. But Scott," she looked at him, her eyes still moist, "no one has ever formally recognized that. Thank you."

"You're welcome, Emma. You are the best at what you do and everyone in the company recognizes that. We're going to need your best. The RRI proposal is coming together and we only have about four weeks to go. Joanne will be contacting you about your role and for some numbers from your perspective. I want you to be part of the pitch team. We need to win this thing, and I want you to prepare your section for next week." He hesitated a moment as if pondering what he was going to say next. "You know, Emma, I haven't shared this with anyone, but I'm worried that we may not be able to win this thing. I know that we're all going to have to stretch to do it."

Emma looked at Scott for a long time. "You know I don't pull too many punches, Scott, so here goes. Until today I would have agreed with you." She reached across the desk and extended her hand to him. "Let's win this together, Scott." He reached over and shook Emma's hand.

After she left, Scott walked to the window and started to cry. He went over to the door and closed it quickly and then went back to the window. Nothing. Nothing in his career had come close to the meaning of his last two decisions. The opportunities of being a manager were awesome and he knew it. It was like Eric said: This job was about people, and his life could be about people. That's where the meaning and purpose could be found. He knew this was not going to be easy, he had a long way to go, but it was the right path for him to be on.

When John found out, he took his new job in stride. There was a bit of that "I-told-you-so." Scott noticed it and acknowledged that John was right and let it go. John had made great inroads with Jameela's group and asked Scott if he would attend the next meeting. Scott was about to ask who would be there but decided against that and asked, "You scope it out, John, and if you think I can add value, I will clear my plate to be there. If you decide that you can handle it I'm very confident that you will advance our needs."

John looked at Scott, as if he didn't hear him correctly. "Okay. I'll take a look at it and get back. I thought you might need to be there."

"No, you understand that area well but, if required call me, and I'll go. But John, I want you to use Emma as a mentor in some areas." He could see the defensiveness in John, but Scott was-n't going to let this one go. "I think that you don't need help in some areas, but in others I want you to get some advice from Emma before going to the client. She's the best we have with some people skills and you can learn a lot from her."

He didn't seem convinced, but that was John. "For a while, John, I want you to get Emma's counsel formally before mate-rials go out to the client. If that is something you can't do let me know and we can discuss it. John you should be in this posi-tion. It has the kind of consistent client contact that suits your talents well. We both know that." Scott added, "Now, Emma has some strategic directions and savvy that are truly excep-tional. If you can find a way to leverage that with your skills, then I know that we will do well."

"Is it a requirement of this job, Scott?"

John clearly didn't like it. Scott had thought about this for a long time. He didn't enjoy his interactions with John but he did recognized his talent more clearly now. He knew John could make a contribution but also believed it would be limited with-out some guidance. "John, I need an exceptionally high level of performance in that role from day one. If I felt we could afford some growing time, I would not be so adamant about this. It's a requirement of the position for at least the first year."

"I think you know I'd rather do it alone."

"Yes, I understand, and I can relate to that."

"When do I start?" John stated.

"Yesterday." They both laughed. "Talk with Emma about the transition and set up a formal mentoring process after RRI. Right now, I need you to work with Emma in whatever way you both decide to get the roles straightened out for the presentation. I've given Joanne some role descriptions, but I expect that you and Emma might refine them to leverage your strengths in the pitch."

"Am I going to the pitch? John asked, surprised.

"Yes. And you're going to be a big part of it. I want our customer to see you and me as the go-to people inside the company. I won't always have time to follow up with them and I want them to feel that if they get either of us they are getting what they need."

John was jumping. This was his area. He could spend all day with a client, seven days a week, and it wouldn't be enough. "Jameela has already made inroads there. She knew someone from Reel to Real from a long time ago and Jameela is great. Can I ask her to be part of the pitch team Scott?"

Scott knew how this conversation would have gone in the past, very differently from his reply now, "Let's win this, John. If you think Jameela can contribute then ask her. Just let me know how you see the roles shaking out before we commit, that's all."

John almost ran out of the office. Giving him the opportunity to shine, front and center, in a client's office—where if he does well he would get the credit directly was like giving an actor a stage, a big bright spotlight to stand in and an audience that he would bring to their feet one way or another. Emma didn't have that need for constant applause and reinforcement. She was more strategic in her approach to clients and liked to see them, but only after much thought and when she was totally buttoned down. But John would work night and day for the chance to look like a star, and you could throw him on the stage and he would pull together something very good, very quickly. Emma's strategy and John's ability to deliver it with flexible, in-the-moment reactions was what they needed to win. Keeping John's ego in check long enough for him to use Emma's brilliance was going to be a balancing act, but Scott was clear in his own mind, nothing less would win.

A week later Jameela called Scott. She sounded surprised but her tone was very friendly. "I don't know what you've done with John lately Scott, but we can't contain his enthusiasm. He wants me in on the pitch, to be there with your team in California. Is that what you want?"

The irony didn't escape Scott. He wondered what Eric must be thinking. "If John asked you, then I have confidence that he believes we can win with you there. I personally would appreciate it, Jameela. I think what you say is always well respected and thought out."

Jameela seemed a bit nervous. "Great, and I think my connections there can help us a bit."

"Okay, Jameela. I asked John to outline the roles clearly for me
and when I see them, let's talk about how to use your talents.
I'm really looking forward to this."

"So am I, Scott. Let's win it."

When Jameela hung up, he realized what he had done. He
was picturing this team. Not *his* team but *this* team in which he
played a significant role, each with their individual talents show-
cased in the right way: Joanne, Emma, John, Jameela and himself. It didn't feel like an all-star cast just a short while ago but
it did now. What had changed? Scott had a lot to do to prepare
for the presentation, but he was getting excited.

He stayed late that evening specifically to see Eric. When Eric
came this time he had aged considerably. It was as if Scott had-
n't seen him in years. His hair was more white than gray, his
face had new creases and his movements appeared slower and
weaker as he reached for the basket.

"Eric, what happened to you?" Scott got out of his chair and
went over to Eric, but the old man would not be helped as he
sat down.

"I'm fine. Haven't you ever seen a man age before?" He smiled as he said it.

"Yes, but not this quickly, Eric." Scott said. "What's happening to you. Why are you here?" and he added, "Who are you?"

Eric stretched his feet out in front of him and crossed his arms as he began to speak in a calm, detached voice. "I spent a long time collecting garbage. Many types of garbage. For most of my life I managed a private garbage collection company. I never found a sense of meaning in either my work or my life. It wasn't until my deathbed," Eric watched Scott's face for a reaction but there was none, "looking back at all the wasted moments, all of my efforts that weren't directed at building something worthwhile for others or myself, that I saw that it didn't have to be that way. I saw it had been my choice, that experience had provided the lessons, and the painful signals, again and again, but I never paid attention. I always moved on, only to run into the same experience around the next corner, too afraid to look clearly at what it might say about me.

"Only when I lay there and knew that my life had minutes left, yes, just minutes, did I realize how I had squandered millions of those precious moments. Only then did I understand that my time never had to be focused on garbage. But that's what I thought my job was about. I should have known it was about people. You can take any element out of business and still call it business, except people. I realized that my job should have been about connecting to others, helping myself and others make sense out of our work. My life could have been about making something worthy of valuable, finite minutes—my own and others' about finding order within the chaos and building community with others. My work should have been about helping others and myself find meaning and purpose in what we invest *our whole lives,* doing."

Eric looked at the tiles in the ceiling. He didn't want to meet Scott's eyes as he spoke in a voice laced with regret. "Don't look back from your deathbed and realize that you believed you were managing something, anything. If you forget you're managing people, you'll lose all meaning in your work and life."

Scott realized why people used the phrase "falling into silence." That is what he felt, like he was falling, the whooshing of air created a feeling of vertigo even as he sat in his chair. The words that used to make sense simply didn't anymore. Eric and Scott sat together for what seemed like a long time.

Scott finally broke the silence: "Then why are you here now? Don't you have an appointment, umm," he hesitated and without moving his head glanced up and pointed toward the ceiling, "upstairs?" Eric started laughing and soon they both were laughing.

When they stopped, Eric answered, "Yes, as a matter of fact I do, shortly." He saw the concern in Scott's face. "Don't worry. I'm almost ready to go. They gave me an option when I was going the last time. I could go on without really experiencing the lessons I was here to get, or they could send me back to learn through helping someone else not make the same mistakes. I was very tired then, Scott. I was ready to sleep for a while before my next experience. So I chose to leave. I was just too tired to face the world again. But then I got the call, so to speak, from you on the dock. When I saw you standing there, it was like looking in the mirror. A wonderful life being wasted, filled with so much garbage. I couldn't go. I told them that I would meet you."

Eric was aging as he spoke. Scott was sure of it. It wasn't like in a bad movie, but whenever Scott looked closely at one of Eric's features it seemed to have changed, slightly but absolutely. Scott asked, "You mean you came back, just for me?"

"Yes."

Scott's eyes teared up as he looked at this tired man in front of him, as he thought of him making a decision from his deathbed.

"It was a decision," he said, as if reading Scott's mind, "to connect, to find meaning in my life. A decision that I needed to make again and again throughout my life. I have gained as much from our encounters as you have. But my time is almost up, Scott, and I have to go soon." He got up slowly, emptied Scott's wastebasket and started walking toward the door.

"You mean I won't see you again, Eric?" Scott couldn't hide his feelings.

"You will, Scott, for a while yet. We have something to complete."

Management Lesson Number Six

Walk softly and carry a big idea!

chapter eleven

Wow !nc.

> "Worse than not having sight is having no vision."
> —*Helen Keller*

Scott realized that the world had not changed, but that for him it was never going to be the same; something was changing, had changed, inside of him. But there was still more to learn.

Walk softly and carry a big idea! He wondered about it as he dressed for work. He felt like he was learning to stop, look and listen more often, to himself and to others. He was learning about the fundamental importance of seeing people clearly, for what they are, with all of their strengths and weaknesses, and their true talents. He had also given up the notion of fixing them. Instead, he would focus on bringing out and leveraging the talents that they had naturally. He could see that chaos could never be eliminated and unleashing his people would naturally create more chaos. But it was in those individually motivated and generated connections, in those beautifully chaotic structures of relationships that, if he could be patient, he would find a new order, an order that built connection and community and ultimately meaning for others, and, as he was finding, for himself.

Scott was growing, making mistakes but truly learning, both from experience and through wisdom how to "walk softly." But what is does it mean to "Walk softly and carry a big idea?"

"Dad." Scott's train of thought went sailing right off its tracks. "Look at this. Mom got it for me yesterday."

Scott got down and sat on the carpet with his son. He took the box from him and looked at its familiar lettering. Replico Inc., it said in large lettering on the side. On the top was a pirate ship, one of their top-selling models. Sabrina would have had to pay retail price for this, was the first thought that first went through his mind. Why didn't she ask him to bring this home from the store at work?

Scott opened the package and pulled out the contents. The instruction pages were colorful, and there was a lot of time and detail in the illustrations and in the history provided on pirates. He knew who had written that—an older woman named Patty, who loved to add stories and lore to the model instructions. She did it in the beginning on her own initiative because she loved pirates and their tales, but later the company made it a standard part of each kit.

"Wow!" Jim exclaimed as he looked at the world that he would soon be immersed in. He loved the models from Replico.

Goose bumps pushed up through Scott's skin. Jim was right: It was "Wow!" That's what the business was about. It wasn't about the models itself: it was about creating the sense of wonder. Actually it was about helping the "Wow!" already inside Jim find expression. That was the big idea; a bigger idea than he had ever had before, a bigger idea than the business had been able to understand, focus resources on consistently communicate. Now he understood the message. People like Patty and others had felt it, but nothing was being done with it, no systems were built to support it, no heart built into the machine. He hugged his son, and they were both called down for breakfast. "Wow is right, son. This is going to be a great model. Let's do it together tonight."

When Scott walked into Bob's office with an idea, it was three weeks before the pitch with RRI. Bob was glad to see Scott and told him he had heard good things about the project from Jameela.

"That's great, Bob. I want to talk to you about that. This is related, but it's bigger than this project." He went on to tell him about Jim opening his Replico pirate model, his insight into what the company was really selling. "If we lose the 'Wow!' Bob, we're out of business and it doesn't matter how exact our models are. If we're going to turn this company one-hundred-and-eighty degrees, then I propose that we go after that directly, and clearly target our talent at creating 'Wow!' every time with every customer."

Bob smiled and sat back. "And when would you like to do this, Scott? Today?"

Scott wasn't sure if he had done the right thing. Perhaps Bob was thinking this was ill-conceived or frivolous, but Scott was sure it was exactly the opposite and went on: "It's getting more and more competitive. The consumer is more and more sophisticated. We have to clearly stake out our ground, our niche, and position the company's benefits with every communication. Our name is our number one means of communicating, Bob, and I just don't think it's working hard enough for us now. We have to create 'Wows,' in our customers, or we lose jobs." Scott was about to continue, but Bob cut him off.

Bob started to reminisce. "I remember when this company got off the ground. That's all it was, Scott, a big idea that drew me and others along with it because it was a larger vision for what was possible. That was the kind of thinking that started me on this road, and I've never lost it. I have a great attachment to the Replico name; but let me think about this."

Scott wasn't surprised. He didn't expect a name change right away. There was great equity in the Replico name and any transition would take a full scale, market-driven process, but he hoped that Bob would consider it. Scott replied, "Thanks, Bob. I think we have an opportunity to revitalize our brand and our company and to bring some of your enthusiasm to a new generation of customers. There was something that I want to get your approval on, though. It may seem like semantics, but I believe it will be important for our pitch and for our team, and it'll provide a focus for RRI."

"What's that?" Bob sat forward in his chair.

"If we get the account, I think we should start a division called Wow !nc. that will handle the entire project from start to finish. It'll be responsible for the entire themed experience and be one hundred percent focused on creating Wow! customer experiences. We'll use our in house talents and partner with the best in the world."

"And who would head up this division operationally, Scott?"

Without a pause Scott said, "Jameela would be the best if she's interested, but I haven't talked to her. I can integrate Wow !nc.'s marketing efforts with the larger company. I understand how to position us better than most, I think, but I believe Jameela would create a sustaining organization, with the systems that would keep us delivering consistently over time. I can make my contribution and it will be significant, but I think running the operations should be hers."

Bob was taken aback. He knew that getting the RRI project work would require a separate team, but the dedication of the resources was going to be a stretch. He also recognized that Jameela was the best candidate, but he was surprised that Scott realized that. He looked at Scott for a while as if seeing something in him for the first time.

Bob replied, "It feels like we're in the start-up phase again. Scott, you can put it into the proposal as long as the ranges I have approved on the budget are respected." He added, "Joanne has been terrific working with our office on those matters. Scott, you've got a very talented team."

Scott had no idea Joanne had been working directly with Bob's office, this pleased him. "Yes, I do, Bob."

"I will see if Jameela wants those added responsibilities when I talk to her next. Good suggestions. Are we going to win the business?"

Scott looked at him and realized with great joy that he meant what he was saying. "They would be crazy not to hire us."

"Good, Scott. Go get it." As Bob shook his hand, Scott realized that they had just formed a different relationship.

The meeting with the team was exciting and nerve racking at the same time. It was a week before their meeting at RRI. They rehearsed the presentation, and Scott told them about Wow !nc. Bob wouldn't have had time to ask Jameela about heading it up, and Scott didn't think it his place to bring it up first. He wondered what Jameela thought as the proposal showed the new division, Wow !nc., focused on creating themed experiences.

"Who do you think Bob would put in charge of that?" Emma asked. She was always the first one to put issues on the table that everyone was thinking about.

"I know that Bob is thinking about that as we speak. Who knows?" Scott replied.

There was a brief silence in the room and then they jumped back into the rehearsal. They were almost but not quite ready. Great content but the presentation was less than stellar. Joanne was by far the most nervous, and she stammered even as they rehearsed. Scott wondered if he had made the right decision. Maybe she's in over her head? Jameela was, as usual, sounding nervous but her thoughts were awesome. He knew that Mary and everyone else at RRI would recognize her out-standing qualities very quickly. John was ready to perform and didn't like to practice, but he went through his paces without showing a bit of his talent, just reading his lines as if he could-n't wait to get out of the office. Others, especially Jameela, looked worried, but Scott knew that there was one place that John never saved any energy and that was in front of the client. John would be fine. Emma quietly smoothed over the areas where they each stumbled and said just the right thing at just the right time. She was a pro, and everyone in the room realized why she was there. Scott was more worried about himself than he was about anyone, even Joanne. He was nervous in a way that he hadn't been since he got married. "And that worked out well," he tried to reassure himself.

The flight to California went quickly. Everyone was concentrating on their own part of the presentation. Jameela was unusually quiet.

Bob didn't want to come along. It was a strategic choice. He had talked to the founder of RRI, Saul Richman, and said he could be there but that he had an amazing team, the people that Mary and others would work with daily. He felt they could win the job and build the relationship properly on their own. Before asking if Saul wanted him to be there, he mentioned the creation of the Wow !nc. division that Jameela had now agreed to lead. Saul was impressed with Bob's confidence and said that he wouldn't be there either but that they could meet separately if the Wow !nc. division—he used the title and it sounded great to Bob—won the contract.

Jameela had been shocked when Bob had told her that Scott recommended her to head up the new division. Both Scott and Bob agreed her unusual ability to win confidence through her performance was more than just important; it was the foundation around which Wow !nc. could grow. She had accepted but didn't have a chance to thank Scott privately before they found themselves on the plane with the team.

As they started to sign in at RRI, Scott looked up at the colorful letters swimming above their heads. It had only been a short time ago that he had been here wondering if they were in over their heads. It seemed like a lifetime. They all joked about it as they squeezed into the opening and sat around the large red donut, waiting for Mary to greet them. Joanne had arrived earlier in order to set up the computer equipment and arrange the meeting room to match, as closely as possible, the setting in which they'd rehearsed the presentation. They would have two hours to change the direction of their company. Their jokes all had a nervous edge, but no one acknowledged or named the elephant that sat in the circle with them.

Mary came down with Joanne. The room must be ready thought Scott, exactly five minutes before they were supposed to present. Mary and Joanne were talking and laughing and somehow that put Scott at ease. Wow! He kept saying it in his head and realizing what a powerful idea it was. The whole team had loved it and the presentation rehearsal had taken on a life of its own that supported the idea.

They were led into the large meeting room. Six people were seated around the table. Everyone was introduced and then Mary said, "Scott, are you ready to go?" Scott's mouth was dry, his heart jumped up into his throat and he almost felt himself choking as he stood up. "Yes. Good morning." He felt his legs lock as he walked stiffly up to the front of the room. Then he thought about it and all felt calm for a moment. He realized what he would say first. He hadn't planned it, or rehearsed this part in their practice session. But what he was about to say calmed him.

"I am very fortunate to work with one of the most talented teams in the world. We would like to win this project, but more importantly, to create something together that neither of our companies could do alone—to create a connection between us that results in something truly spectacular. Let me tell you a short story about something that I learned from a teacher of mine—my son." Scott was on a roll, and win or lose, he was going to drain himself and give it every honest bit of energy he could. He almost had them in tears as he described the insight into his own work he had gained by listening to his son, by really paying attention to the moment. He told them about the new division that would be formed to lead this project and support their efforts. He looked at Jameela and she winked at him. She knew. He then sat back down and let the team take over.

They blew the client away. As he watched he began not only to intellectually understand the "walk softly and carry a big idea" message but to see its impact on others. Joanne didn't show a bit of her nervousness, only Jameela seemed nervous, as always, but it was clear that she was respected right away for her brilliance. John dazzled them and only got better as they challenged the team, and Emma smoothed out the rough edges for the rest of the team, as always. She also jumped in and took one of the toughest questions herself, when the rest of the team hesitated.

He could feel the truth in the message now, "Walk softly and carry a big idea!" he had seen it change his world. When he believed that a different brighter future was not only possible, but worthy of his and others efforts; when he sensed new possibilities in his nerve endings; when he carried a big idea inside himself first then others would almost magically follow. But only, Scott knew, if he had the strength to keep believing when others doubted. He could throw away the stick he had tried to use to keep people in a constant straight line. He now had a much more powerful tool, something that everyone, employees, customers and he was craving for: purpose, contribution, passion; and if it was a large enough idea, then each would find and create their own meaning through their connections with each other and the experience.

By the time they had finished, Scott couldn't contain himself. Whether they won or lost this one, he knew in his heart it didn't matter. They would win their share, with this team firing on all cylinders. Who could stop them?

They celebrated together late into the evening, each congratulating the other. Jameela thanked Scott, in front of the others, who were all surprised, for recommending her for the head operations person for the Wow !nc. division. Scott would remember that night for the rest of this life.

chapter twelve

A Treasure Chest

"Twenty years from now you will be more dissatisfied by the things that you didn't do than by the ones that you did do. So throw off the bowlines. Sail away from the safe harbor. Catch the trade winds in your sails. Explore... Dream... Discover..."
—*Mark Twain*

Scott needed to get work early this morning. It wasn't something he could explain to Sabrina. He got up at five and was at work by five-thirty. He knew that Eric would not show up during the day, and Scott was not going to be working late that night. The morning was his last chance to say goodbye.

He sat down at his desk and looked at the papers strewn about. His desk was a mess. He settled back into his chair and took a deep breath. He felt satisfied. For the first time in a long time he felt full. Present. Without a need to run from here to there. Scott pulled out a piece of paper. Very slowly he began to write something. Just as he was finishing, he heard a rustling outside his door. He knew it would be Eric, and soon the janitor's large peaceful body framed the doorway. Scott grabbed the paper he was working on and crunched it into a ball, as if he had been caught doing something he shouldn't, and tossed it into the wastebasket. There was a long silence. Eric began to smile. It lit up his whole face and make his eyes twinkle. His smile was infectious, and Scott began to smile as well.

Scott broke the silence. "This doesn't seem like enough, Eric, but thank you, my friend."

Eric's smile seemed to expand. "Scott. You were ready to learn and move beyond your pain. It was always up to you." He reached for Scott's basket. For old time's sake, Scott assumed. They both knew that Eric would not be coming back again.

Eric was about to empty the basket when he noticed that there was only one paper in it, crunched up in a ball. Eric looked up for a moment and then sat down. Eric slowly reached in the wastebasket, his aging back not bending as easily as it once had, pulled the crinkled and rumpled paper out, and put the basket down. Scott watched him take great care as he spread the paper flat on top of Scott's desk, holding it with his left hand and smoothing it firmly but gently with the thick side of his right hand. He mouthed the words to himself, savoring them, as if he were enjoying a rich, aged spirit, his palate able to detect every nuance of the journey that had brought these words here.

There were no more words left to say. Eric rose first and slowly started moving toward the door. Scott followed. He knew that he wouldn't see Eric again. Eric turned and put out his hand. Scott wrapped his arms around Eric, hugging him and thanking him again.

Eric didn't say anything as he walked down the hall. His gait was slowing even as he walked. Scott watched him turn the corner around the cubicles and then disappear.

The call came in toward the middle of the morning. By the time he said hello, Joanne had the whole team gathered in his doorway. He looked at them and realized how proud he was of them all.

"Yessssss!" he yelled at the top of his lungs, and his whole team started whooping and yelling in the hall. Others in the company were already congratulating the team as he made his way out of his office. They all hugged and laughed and cheered, but Scott said he had to go to an appointment that afternoon. He was out the door quickly.

Within minutes Scott was driving to the beach. I only have a few minutes, he thought, as he called Sabrina to let her know what he was going to do. He also told her they had won the job, but that came second. There was a moment's silence, then, "I love you, Scott."

Scott stopped at the beach, then he went home. Jim was just coming out the front door with Sabrina ready for the walk back to school for the afternoon. Scott jumped out of his car.

"Jim! Jim!" he blurted out as he leapt from the car, the door still ajar and the car sitting at an angle almost in the middle of Boardwalk Drive.

Jim didn't know what to do or say. He hadn't seen his father like this for a long time. Maybe never. "What is it, Dad?"

Jim sounded almost worried and Scott, despite sensing the child's concern, perhaps because of it, continued in the same excited tone, "You wouldn't believe what I just heard!"

"What, Dad?" This time Jim seemed more curious than concerned, and Scott felt a bit of relief.

"I was just down at the beach. I stopped there to take a walk, and I heard them. I heard them. I finally heard them, Jim."

"Who, Dad? Who did you hear?"

"The pirates, son. I was down beside the Leuty Lifeguard Station, and I overheard these two pirates arguing over who would come back and claim their treasure."

Jim was excited now. He looked at his dad, and then his mom, as if wondering what to do and then he asked, "Was the one with the black hair and the fuses sticking out of it, was he there, Dad?"

"Yes, Jim, he was, and he said that a treasure map is buried down by the lifeguard station." Scott glanced at Sabrina. She was smiling, her eyes were misty.

"Dad! Dad!" Jim was almost too excited to talk now. "Could we go look for it tomorrow when there's no school?"

Scott pretended to be serious. "No, Jim. I'm sorry," he paused, Jim's shoulder's almost slumped, "we had better do it today before some scurvy dog finds it before us treasure hunters!" Jim jumped over to Scott and then back to his mother, "I better get my eye patch, matey," he yelled, "and my sand toys for digging, right Dad?"

As Scott stood up from his crouching position, he replied, "Yes son, that would be a good thing, in case we find it." Jim ran in the house, and Sabrina came over and wrapped her arms around Scott. She pressed her cheek to his and held it there a long time. "You didn't shave this morning, Captain." They both laughed and Jim came flying out the door with his eye patch on the side of his head, a small toy telescope bouncing in his sand bucket in one hand and his sand shovel in the other. "Gotta set sail, lassie. Jim-ladd and I have some treasure huntin' to do. Keep a candle burnin' in the window. Yer men will be home in no time."

"Good to hear, Captain," Sabrina laughed. "Yo pirate!" She continued. Jim turned around. "Do your coat up down at the beach, okay? Those treasure huntin' winds can give a pirate a nasty cold."

"I will, Mom."

Scott pulled the car to the side of the road, got out and took the shovel from Jim. The little boy's small hand slipped easily and quickly into his. Sabrina watched her two men walk down to the end of the street and turn through the laneway where they could cross to the beach.

"The pirates pointed toward the lifeguard station. The map must be around there, son. Let's start there."

Jim walked toward the station and once there he started to scrounge around in the sand with an intensity that surprised Scott. He knew his son was bright and that he was easily able to understand that pirates were not at the beach, but he was at the same time able to understand that they were. "What a wonderful talent," thought Scott as his son dug in the sand, turning over rocks and sticks, occasionally finding something which he would examine closely and then throw over his shoulder, "to be able to see so much when many see so little."

Scott moved toward a sharp rock and leaned against it, rubbing the sand under his foot until an old paper partially stuck up. He waited for Jim to glance up and when he did Scott walked down the beach as if looking in another place for the map.

"Dad! Dad! Look at this!" He had seen the paper. Scott came back as Jim pulled it out. "It's a treasure map!" Jim yelled. He uncurled the paper and laid it flat on the sand. Jim could hardly stand still, and Scott wondered if they could make it to a bathroom in time if his son had to go in a hurry.

"Look, Dad!" He pointed to the dotted line that ran along the edge of the beach, through one set of rocks arranged in a circle, turning to another set of rocks stacked three high, then fifteen giant paces, Scott read to Jim, to a place where a giant X was made in the sand.

Jim stood up and moved the eye patch over his left eye. He picked up the telescope and surveyed the beach. "Is all safe, Captain?" Scott asked his son.

"Aye, aye, Dad. Let's go."

They traced the route laid out in the map. When they found the circle of rocks Jim ran around it faster and faster until he dropped. Then when they found the stacked rocks, he turned and started counting, taking his own giant steps to where the X would be. Scott, quickly realizing that the boy would be only about a third of the way there by the time he hit fifteen paces, ran over and picked him up, saying, "Let's do this together, Captain." Holding his little pirate high, he took giant step after giant step until they counted fifteen. Looking down from way up in the crow's nest, the little Captain was for the first time, speechless. He could see, dug into the sand, a clear and large X. Both pirates stood for a moment.

"I think you should start the digging, Jim," Scott said. "You were the one to find the pirates in the first place and you found the map." He placed Jim on the ground and ran back to get the shovel where they'd left it.

Jim started to dig. He had to work at it, and Scott worried that someone might have come by since he had buried the treasure. Jim kept digging hard. Scott looked at his son while he worked, and saw the determination in his young eyes. He could feel the energy and the life that was in him. Scott wanted to grab his son, to hold him and never let him go. He wanted to tell him how much he loved him and loved the world he brought with him; the world that he had created and had helped Scott to see. Scott wondered if he could ever be more proud of his son or more humbled by this gift from God than he was at this moment.

"Dad! Oh Dad!" Scott could hear his shovel hitting something. Jim fell to his knees and started brushing sand away with his hands. The brownish texture showed through first. As he pulled sand away, the round surface of the lid was revealed and soon Jim had his hands around the bottom of the treasure chest and was yanking it out. Scott moved the sand away from its sides, and Jim's final tug brought the small chest out with a whoosh.

Jim leapt to his feet and ran around and around not saying a word. Then he fell to his knees and opened the lid. Inside were two small books on pirates, chocolate gold coins and shiny rocks, a jack knife and some twisted rope. Jim wouldn't discover the smaller compartments on the side until later at home.

"Dad! Dad! Mom's not going to believe it!" He held the box up in the air and jumped up and down. "It's real, Dad. It's real."

The blue sky faded to white as it touched the horizon of sparkling water. Against the backdrop of the beautiful August day played the silhouettes of father and son, their joyous shadows in the mid-day light moving and dancing in the sun-bleached sand. Scott tucked the crumpled paper deeper into his pocket, and pulled his son to him. He felt the tug of his son's small strong arms enveloping him. A cool breeze softly wafted in over them both and then gently disappeared. Tears began streaming down Scott's face. "Yes, son. More real than I ever could have imagined."

Management Lesson Number Seven

What is real?

People are real.

Whatever ties or figments of ties, or hints or spirits of ties that connect people or life itself — they are Real.

Whatever meaning people find in their relationships, work, in their own unique experience of living — that is real.

Everything else is an illusion.